CONSUMER HEALTH
Activities

Stephen L. Brown, PhD

LARNE

Larne Publishing
Murphysboro, Illinois, USA
2010

Consumer Health Activities
Copyright 2010 by Stephen L Brown.

Published by:
Larne Publishing
7168 Highway 127
Murphysboro, IL 62966-5814
(618) 684-8587
larne@inbox.com

Consumer Health Activities / by Stephen L. Brown, PhD
Includes table of contents and subject index

ISBN-13: 978-0-615-34851-3
1. Medical care. 2. Health products. 3. Consumer education.

Printed in the United States of America

Cover design by Russell McMullin (www.mcmullincreative.com)

About the Author

Stephen L Brown, PhD, is an Associate Professor of Health Education at Southern Illinois University Carbondale, where he teaches and mentors undergraduate, MPH and PhD students in community and school health education. He has taught Consumer Health and Consumer Behavior courses for more than a decade at two universities. Dr. Brown has a PhD in Community and Public Health Education from the University of Maryland, an MS in Exercise Science and Wellness from Arizona State University, and a BS in Business Administration and Marketing from Brigham Young University. Dr. Brown has published dozens of articles in national and international journals of health promotion and presented in numerous conferences. He also conducts research related to adolescent health behavior, college health behavior, and emotional health. In addition to Consumer Health courses, he teaches Personal Health, Health Behavior, Stress Management, Emotional Health, Substance Use, and various theory and methodology courses. Prior to working in public health and health education, Dr. Brown did consumer marketing and merchandising for an international retailer.

Acknowledgements

I appreciate the advice given by several of my colleagues at Southern Illinois University during the development and editing of this work. I am also grateful to many students over the years who have been *guinea pigs* for several activities and given valuable suggestions for making them more useful and "fun."

Dedication

To Jana, who has put up with me for more than 20 years; and Joshua, Noah, Seth, Faith, Joy, and Adam, who make life interesting.

To the Reader

Consumer Health is not a topic that is entirely new to you. You likely have been making decisions that affect your health and health care for years. Nor is it a topic that you forget once you close the back cover or turn in your final exam. It is a part of your life that you will confront many times throughout the years and likely more frequently the older you get. Consumer Health does not refer to a narrow academic discipline, but rather a broad collection of topics that deal with the decisions we make as consumers, the behaviors we practice, the products we use, the professionals we choose, the services we seek, and the financial decisions we make. All of which affect our health or the health of our loved ones.

This is not your typical textbook. It is not about reading and memorizing, but about doing. It is properly called an activity book because you must take an active part in the learning. And what's more, most of these activities will be personal, allowing you to learn things about yourself, your health, your family, the health care you have available to you, and the choices you will have now and in the future.

This is not "busy work," but it will require some work beyond reading. Depending on the activity, you will be talking to professionals, interviewing family, experimenting on yourself, analyzing your choices, or researching on the Internet. These activities have been tested by college students who have found that they not only provide very personal learning experiences, but that they are also fun.

Although it is not possible to address every health decision you will make in life, this activity book is designed to provide a broad survey of the health issues consumers face. These include the health care marketplace, advertising, conventional medicine, alternative medicine, emergencies and first aid, diet, fitness, weight control, common diseases, drugs, health and beauty aids, reproductive health, end of life issues, and financial issues such as insurance.

If you are using the book as part of a class, your instructor will likely assign you the most relevant activities and have you submit a worksheet, a typed analysis or reflection paper. However, the book can be highly personal and I encourage you to pursue any activities for which you have personal interest or need, assigned or not.

Stephen L. Brown, PhD

For the Instructor

Consumer Health is a topic that cannot be thoroughly understood simply by reading a textbook. Students are more likely to understand and remember when they apply what they learn.

This book is designed for college-level courses in Consumer Health or Personal Health, but may also be useful in Health Education, Consumer Education, Home Economics, Community Health, or Health Promotion courses. Most of the activities would also be appropriate for high school-level Health Education and Consumer Education classes.

The boo can be used as a supplement to a conventional chapter-based text of readings. However, many instructors will choose to make this the primary text, covering the didactive material in class. Although primarily designed to be individual, many of the activities can be adapted as in-class lessons or group exercises; particularly Activities1-8, 15-16, 24-26, 28-36, 39, 44, 50, 54, 58-60.

Approximately 1/3 of the activities will require students to have access to a computer and the Internet to lookup information, read descriptions, or complete personal inventories. All of the Internet addresses were accurate and working as of printing; however, some may have changed since publication. I have tried to give sufficient information to find the addresses again if necessary and substitute sites when available.

Most of the activities have been designed to be completed in an hour or less at one sitting; however, some of them will require more time. Some will also require pre-work such as phone calls, visits to local establishments or interviews. Students will need to plan ahead for some of these activities and budget their time accordingly. Before making assignments, instructors should work through the activities themselves to get a feel for how long they will take, how difficult they are, and what lead time they will require. More challenging activities should likely be worth more points.

Please don't hesitate to contact me if you have any questions or if you have suggestions for the next edition.

Stephen L. Brown, PhD (s.brown@inbox.com)

Contents

Part Four—Safety

Part Five—Diet and Nutrition

Part Six—Fitness and Weight Management

Part Seven—Chronic Disease

Part One
Consumer Behavior

Activity 1—Health Behaviors

The Centers for Disease Control and Prevention (CDC) have been using surveillance tools for years to collect health related data in the United States. Tools are used to measure injuries, hospitals visits, chronic disease prevalence and the spread of infectious disease. Some tools are designed to measure behaviors that increase or decrease risk for various diseases.

One such tool is the Youth Risk Behavior Survey, typically given to high school age youth every other year. It monitors six categories of health-risk behaviors, including those that contribute to unintentional injuries and violence: tobacco use, alcohol and other drug use, sexual behaviors that contribute to unintended pregnancy and sexually transmitted diseases (STDs), unhealthy dietary behaviors, and physical inactivity. It also monitors the prevalence of obesity and asthma. In 1995, the CDC expanded its surveillance by measuring self-report of these and related behaviors on college campuses. This was called the National College Health Risk Behavior Survey (NCHRBS). This activity will give you some exposure to the types of behaviors of greatest concern for college students.

Directions:

First.　　Complete the multi-part NCHRBS questionnaire that follows (your instructor will not share your responses with anyone and your answers will not affect your grade).

Second.　Compare your answers with national trends for the NCHRBS for the selected behaviors that are given at the end.

Third.　　In one page, discuss why you believe national averages were higher or lower than your answers for various behaviors. Describe what you could do to lower your own risks.

National College Health Risk Behavior Survey

Injury-related

How often do you wear a seat belt when riding in a car driven by someone else?	
	Never
	Rarely
	Sometimes
	Most of the time
√	Always

How often do you wear a seat belt when driving a car?	
	I do not drive a car
	Never wear a seat belt
	Rarely wear a seat belt
	Sometimes wear a seat belt
	Most of the time wear a seat belt
√	Always wear a seat belt

When you rode a bicycle during the past 12 months, how often did you wear a helmet?	
	I did not ride a bicycle during the past 12 months
√	Never wore a helmet
	Rarely wore a helmet
	Sometimes wore a helmet
	Most of the time wore a helmet
	Always wore a helmet

When you went boating or swimming during the past 12 months, how often did you drink alcohol?	
√	I did not go boating or swimming during the past 12 months
	Never drank alcohol
	Rarely drank alcohol
	Sometimes drank alcohol
	Most of the time drank alcohol
	Always drank alcohol

During the past 30 days, how many times did you ride in a car or other vehicle driven by someone who had been drinking alcohol?

√	0 times
	1 time
	2 or 3 times
	4 or 5 times
	6 or more times

During the past 30 days, how many times did you drive a car or other vehicle when you had been drinking alcohol?

√	0 times
	1 time
	2 or 3 times
	4 or 5 times
	6 or more times

During the past 30 days, on how many days did you carry a weapon such as a gun, knife, or club? Do not count carrying a weapon as part of your job.

√	0 days
	1 day
	2 or 3 days
	4 or 5 days
	6 or more days

During the past 12 months, how many times were you in a physical fight?

√	0 times
	1 time
	2 or 3 times
	4 or 5 times
	6 or 7 times
	8 or 9 times
	10 or 11 times
	12 or more times

During the past 12 months, with whom did you fight?	
	A total stranger
	A friend or someone I know
	A boyfriend, girlfriend, or date
	My spouse or domestic partner
	A parent, brother, sister, or other family member
×	Other

During the past 12 months, did you ever seriously consider attempting suicide?	
	Yes
√	No

During the past 12 months, did you make a plan about how you would attempt suicide?	
	Yes
√	No

During the past 12 months, how many times did you actually attempt suicide?	
√	0 times
	1 time
	2 or 3 times
	4 or 5 times
	6 or more times

Tobacco, alcohol, and other drugs

Have you ever tried cigarette smoking, even one or two puffs?	
	Yes
√	No

During the past 30 days, on how many days did you smoke cigarettes?	
√	0 days
	1 or 2 days
	3 to 5 days
	6 to 9 days
	10 to 19 days
	20 to 29 days
	All 30 days

During the past 30 days, on how many days did you use chewing tobacco or snuff, such as Redman, Levi Garrett, Beechnut, Skoal, Skoal Bandits, or Copenhagen?	
√	0 days
	1 or 2 days
	3 to 5 days
	6 to 9 days
	10 to 19 days
	20 to 29 days
	All 30 days

During the past 30 days, on how many days did you have at least one drink of alcohol?	
√	0 days
	1 or 2 days
	3 to 5 days
	6 to 9 days
	10 to 19 days
	20 to 29 days
	All 30 days

During the past 30 days, on how many days did you have 5 or more drinks of alcohol in a row, that is, within a couple of hours?	
√	0 days
	1 day
	2 days
	3 to 5 days
	6 to 9 days
	10 to 19 days
	20 or more days

During your life, how many times have you used marijuana?	
√	0 times
	1 or 2 times
	3 to 9 times
	10 to 19 times
	20 to 39 times
	40 to 99 times
	100 or more times

During the past 30 days, how many times did you use marijuana?
✓ 0 times
1 or 2 times
3 to 9 times
10 to 19 times
20 to 39 times
40 or more times

During your life, how many times have you used any form of cocaine, including powder, crack, or freebase?
✓ 0 times
1 or 2 times
3 to 9 times
10 to 19 times
20 to 39 times
40 to 99 times
100 or more times

During the past 30 days, how many times did you use any form of cocaine, including powder, crack, or freebase?
✓ 0 times
1 or 2 times
3 to 9 times
10 to 19 times
20 to 39 times
40 or more times

During your life, how many times have you sniffed glue, or breathed the contents of aerosol spray cans, or inhaled any paints or sprays to get high?
✓ 0 times
1 or 2 times
3 to 9 times
10 to 19 times
20 to 39 times
40 to 99 times
100 or more times

During your life, how many times have you used any other type of illegal drug, such as LSD, PCP, ecstasy, mushrooms, speed, ice, or heroin?

- [✓] 0 times
- [ ] 1 or 2 times
- [ ] 3 to 9 times
- [ ] 10 to 19 times
- [ ] 20 to 39 times
- [ ] 40 to 99 times
- [ ] 100 or more times

During the past 30 days, how many times have you used any other type of illegal drug, such as LSD, PCP, ecstasy, mushrooms, speed, ice, or heroin?

- [✓] 0 times
- [ ] 1 or 2 times
- [ ] 3 to 9 times
- [ ] 10 to 19 times
- [ ] 20 to 39 times
- [ ] 40 or more times

Sexual behaviors

During the past 30 days, how many times did you have sexual intercourse?

- [✓] 0 times
- [ ] 1 time
- [ ] 2 or 3 times
- [ ] 4 to 9 times
- [ ] 10 to 19 times
- [ ] 20 or more times

During the past 30 days, how often did you or your partner use a condom?

- [✓] I have not had sexual intercourse during the past 30 days
- [ ] Never used a condom
- [ ] Rarely used a condom
- [ ] Sometimes used a condom
- [ ] Most of the time used a condom
- [ ] Always used a condom

	Did you drink alcohol or use drugs before you had sexual intercourse the last time?
√	I have never had sexual intercourse
	Yes
	No

	The last time you had sexual intercourse, what method did you or your partner use to prevent pregnancy?
	No method was used to prevent pregnancy
	Birth control pills
	Condoms
	Withdrawal
	Some other method
√	Not sure

	How many times have you been pregnant or gotten someone pregnant?
√	0 times
	1 time
	2 or more times
	Not sure

	During your life, have you ever been forced to have sexual intercourse against your will?
	Yes
√	No

Dietary behaviors

	Yesterday, how many times did you eat fruit?
	0 times
	1 time
√	2 times
	3 or more times

	Yesterday, how many times did you drink fruit juice?
	0 times
	1 time
√	2 times
	3 or more times

Yesterday, how many times did you eat green salad?
☐ 0 times
☑ 1 time
☐ 2 times
☐ 3 or more times

Yesterday, how many times did you eat cooked vegetables?
☐ 0 times
☐ 1 time
☑ 2 times
☐ 3 or more times

Yesterday, how many times did you eat hamburger, hot dogs, or sausage?
☑ 0 times
☐ 1 time
☐ 2 times
☐ 3 or more times

Yesterday, how many times did you eat french fries or potato chips?
☐ 0 times
☑ 1 time
☐ 2 times
☐ 3 or more times

Yesterday, how many times did you eat cookies, doughnuts, pie, or cake?
☐ 0 times
☑ 1 time
☐ 2 times
☐ 3 or more times

How do you describe your weight?
☐ Very underweight
☐ Slightly underweight
☑ About the right weight
☐ Slightly overweight
☐ Very overweight

	Which of the following are you trying to do about your weight?
	Lose weight
	Gain weight
√	Stay the same weight
	I am not trying to do anything about my weight

	During the past 30 days, which of the following did you try to lose weight or to keep from gaining weight?
	Dieting
√	Exercise
	Vomiting or laxatives
	Diet pills
	None of these

Physical activity

	On how many of the past 7 days did you exercise or participate in sports activities for at least 20 minutes that made you sweat and breathe hard, such as basketball, jogging, swimming laps, tennis, fast bicycling, or similar aerobic activities?
	0 days
	1 day
	2 days
	3 days
	4 days
√	5 days
	6 days
	7 days

	On how many of the past 7 days did you do stretching exercises, such as toe touching, knee bending, or leg stretching?
	0 days
	1 day
	2 days
√	3 days
	4 days
	5 days
	6 days
	7 days

On how many of the past 7 days did you do exercises to strengthen or tone your muscles, such as push-ups, sit-ups, or weight lifting?	
	0 days
√	1 day
	2 days
	3 days
	4 days
	5 days
	6 days
	7 days

On how many of the past 7 days did you walk or bicycle for at least 30 minutes at a time? (Include walking or bicycling to or from class or work.)	
	0 days
	1 day
	2 days
	3 days
	4 days
√	5 days
	6 days
	7 days
	Other

Other

On which of the following health topics have you ever received information from your college or university?	
	Tobacco use prevention
√	Alcohol and other drug use prevention
	Violence prevention
	Injury prevention and safety
	Suicide prevention
	Pregnancy prevention
	Sexually transmitted disease (STD) prevention
	Dietary behaviors and nutrition
	Physical activity and fitness

Selected Results from the National College Health Risk Behavior Survey
(% of Undergraduate College Students Who Engaged in Health Risk Behaviors)

Behaviors	18–24 years	>24 years	Total
Injury Related			
Rarely or never used seat belts	11.1	7.8	10.2
Drove after drinking alcohol	27.8	26.7	27.4
Carried a weapon (gun, knife, or club)	8.5	7.3	8.0
Participated in a physical fight	13.2	4.8	10.2
Seriously considered attempting suicide	11.4	8.3	10.3
Tobacco and Drugs			
Current cigarette use	28.8	28.7	29.0
Current episodic heavy drinking	41.5	22.0	34.5
Current marijuana use	17.3	8.3	14.0
Lifetime cocaine use	6.6	28.1	14.4
Sexual Activity			
Ever had sexual intercourse	79.5	97.8	86.1
6 or more sex partners during lifetime	25.7	49.6	34.5
Condom use during last sexual intercourse	37.7	18.5	29.6
Diet and Weight			
Overweight	15.5	28.8	20.5
Exercised to lose weight or prevent weight	53.4	54.0	53.6
Ate 5 or more servings of fruits & vegetables	25.0	28.5	26.3
Physical Activity			
Vigorous physical activity	41.8	30.6	37.6
Moderate physical activity	20.2	18.1	19.5
Strengthening exercises	33.4	23.5	29.9

Full results at: *http://www.cdc.gov/mmwr/preview/mmwrhtml/00049859.htm*

Activity 2—What's Required for Proof?

This activity will help you understand cause-and-effect relationships. How can you tell whether an action causes a certain result or whether the two are simply related? In other words, how can you prove that a particular behavior causes a health problem or that a remedy causes improvement?

Directions:

A) Sir Austin Bradford Hill, the famous British statistician, proposed a list of criteria necessary to prove that an event causes a disease or that a treatment causes a positive outcome. You can read more about these criteria at: *http://www.drabruzzi.com/hills_criteria_of_causation.htm*

Short summary of Criteria

TEMPORAL RELATIONSHIP—if **A** is thought to cause **B**, then **A** must always precede **B** in time. *Example: Does scratching lead to itching or does itching lead to scratching? What's the true temporal sequence?*

STRENGTH OF THE RELATIONSHIP—not only must there be a cause-effect relationship, but that relationship should be of a great enough magnitude to have practical importance. *Example: If having weekly teeth cleanings lowered risk of gingivitis 1% more than semi-annual cleanings, would that be a strong enough relationship to justify the expense and effort?*

DOSE-RESPONSE RELATIONSHIP—if **A** is thought to cause **B**, then increasing **A** should lead to more **B** and decreasing **A** should lead to less **B**. *For example: If eating an extra 3500 calories leads to gaining a pound of body fat, then eating 7000 calories should lead to gaining 2 pounds of fat.*

CONSISTENCY OF FINDINGS—is the cause-effect assumption based on a single study or is there a pattern across multiple studies? *Example: If a physician reports to the CDC that a patient had symptoms of food poisoning after drinking* Pepsi, *does this mean* Pepsi *causes food poisoning or is it just a coincidence? What if dozens of physicians across the country report the same thing?*

PLUASIBILITY—is the relationship logical or physiologically plausible, in other words, consistent with our current understanding of the world? *Example: If a scientist found that washing with warm water increases risk for skin cancer, the rest of the scientific community would be skeptical because there is no plausible explanation for this link. However, this criterion is tricky because occasionally, it's our understanding of the world that is in error.*

NO OTHER EXPLANATIONS—we can only assume a cause-effect relationships if we are sure there are no other possible explanations. *Example: There is a famous finding that if you go to a playground and randomly test children on achievement tests, the taller children will score better. Are taller children smarter? Of course, the answer is that taller children are also usually older.*

B) Next, visit each of the websites listed on the following page and read the short articles *(if any website is not working, simply skip it and do those that work).*

- **Iodine 131 and cancer**--
  http://www.cdc.gov/nceh/radiation/hanford/htdsweb/pdf/htds_aag.pdf

- **Baldness and heart disease**--
  http://articles.mercola.com/sites/articles/archive/2000/01/30/baldness-heart-disease.aspx

- **Dairy foods and bone health**--
  http://www.ajcn.org/cgi/content/abstract/72/3/681

- **Smoking and stress**--
  http://www.planetpsych.com/zPsychology_101/substance/smoking_stress.htm

- **Bras and breast cancer**--
  http://www.cancer.org/docroot/MED/content/MED_6_1x_Underwire_Bras.asp

- **Vasectomies and cancer**--
  http://cancerweb.ncl.ac.uk/cancernet/600326.html

C) Use the checklist that follows and decide whether the behavior/exposure causes the disease/health condition by identifying which criteria are met for each study.

Criteria for Establishing Cause-Effect Relationship CHECKLIST

	Temporal Relationship	Strength of Association	Dose-Response Relationship	Consistency of Findings	Plausibility	No Alternative Explanations
Iodine 131 & Cancer						
Baldness & Heart Disease						
Dairy Foods & Bone Health						
Smoking & Stress						
Bras & Breast Cancer						
Vasectomies & Cancer						

D) After completing the checklist, in one page, discuss any findings that surprised you and identify which criteria seem to be the most misunderstood in your opinion.

Activity 3—Why We're Deceived

Being human, we often become emotional when it concerns our health. Even intelligent and well-educated individuals can sometimes make unwise decisions about their own health care. This activity will teach you to recognize some of the common myths patients believe about health care and to think of reasons these beliefs should be avoided.

Directions:

The table that follows contains common health care beliefs regarding either conventional medicine or alternative medicine. In many instances, these beliefs are in error or are applied too broadly. Imagine you are talking to family members or friends who hold the particular beliefs in question.

For each statement, give a response to counter the reasoning and demonstrate how it can be in error. If you personally agree with the statement or cannot think of a response, look up information online or in a textbook about the issue to develop a response.

Common Health Care Myths Worksheet

	What even intelligent people have said:	How would you respond?
1	I have a college degree and have read the reports they gave me, I think I could tell if it were bogus.	Example answer: *Some deceptive marketers intentionally design their sales materials and websites to resemble credible research documents or reports*
2	Nothing my regular doctor has done helps; why not try this alternative approach?	
3	Why should I depend on my doctor to solve my problems, when I could use this product to take control of my own health and save money?	

	What even intelligent people have said:	How would you respond?
4	Why would I want to put synthetic drugs in my body and have all the negative side effects, when I can simply take this all-natural product?	
5	I know other people who have tried this treatment and their symptoms are completely gone?	
6	The approach they use to deal with my condition is unique and not yet available through regular doctors' offices.	

	What even intelligent people have said:	How would you respond?
7	My doctor was rude and didn't seem concerned about me or my problem.	
8	The advertisement cited a lot of statistics and other people swear by it.	
9	Medical treatments are often harsh and the human body prefers gentle, natural approaches that help the body heal itself.	

Activity 4—Internet Health Information

The Internet is arguably the most popular source for information in the United States and other countries. Today, many people also use the Internet to find health information. Some of the health information online is quite useful, but some of it is unreliable. The problem is that it is sometimes difficult to distinguish fact from fallacy. This assignment will teach you to use critical questions to analyze the credibility of health information available on the Internet.

Directions:

A) *Select one of the following health conditions to research:*
- *Fatigue and energy level*
- *Quick or easy weight loss*
- *Hair loss*
- *Skin or hair quality*
- *Big muscles*
- *Breast or penis enhancement*
- *Poor memory*
- *Toxin cleansing*

B) *Using a popular Internet search engine (e.g. Google, Yahoo), locate two web sites promoting information or remedies for your selected health condition. Select one site that you suspect may contain some misinformation and a second site you believe has credible information.*

C) *Once you have located your two websites, complete the worksheets on the following pages--one for each site.*

Website Credibility Worksheet—Site 1

1. What is the URL (web address)?

   http://www.diagnose-me.com/cond/C313706.html

2. What is the website intended to do (educate, sell, etc.)?

   educate and sell

3. Who has produced or authored the website? What are their credentials?

   Doctors and other staff working remotely across the U.S. & the rest of the world.

4. How often is it updated?

   started in 2002, last update was sept 20, 2010

5. Is it linked to other reputable sources? List them.

   There are no links to other reputable sources

6. What citations does it give for claims? Where do they come from?

   There are no citations.

7. Does it make any questionable statements or exaggerated claims? (Examples: everyone needs this product, can cause dramatic changes, can cure something, breakthroughs, has scare tactics, etc)

   Offers Computer Analysis, standard report and full report. No need to rush to the doctor when you can do an analysis on the computer to be sent to your doctor.

8. What is the truth? Research the truth about the condition and how it can be treated and compare the truth to what the site claims (try sources such as MedlinePlus, NIH, CDC, MayoClinic, etc.)

   From NIH, poor memory can be treated with Vitamin B12, which is a nutrient that helps keep the body's nerve and blood cells healthy & prevents a type of anemia called megaloblastic anemia that makes people tired & weak.

This site is trying to help you by asking specific questions to help doctors figure out what you have through the symptoms that you list.

Website Credibility Worksheet—Site 2

1. What is the URL (web address)?

   http://en. wikipedia. org/ wiki/ Memory — loss

2. What is the website intended to do (educate, sell, etc.)?

   educate

3. Who has produced or authored the website? What are their credentials?

   People of all ages and different cultural backgrounds
   can add and edit the article.

4. How often is it updated?

   Weekly.

5. Is it linked to other reputable sources? List them.

   No, there are no links to other reputable
   sources

6. What citations does it give for claims? Where do they come from?

   There are other citations listed

7. Does it make any questionable statements or exaggerated claims? (Examples: everyone needs this product, can cause dramatic changes, can cure something, breakthroughs, has scare tactics, etc)

   It tells you the symptoms for memory loss,
   prevention of being forgetful, and how it can be
   treated.

8. What is the truth? Research the truth about the condition and how it can be treated and compare the truth to what the site claims (try sources such as MedlinePlus, NIH, CDC, MayoClinic, etc.)

   This site doesn't really state a treatment
   for memory loss, although family support
   may play an important role in treating
   memory loss.

D) *In one page, discuss what you have learned.*

I've learned that there are many different sources that you can get your information from. Some sites are very helpful and gives the information that you are looking for while some other sites let people of all ages (wikipedia) to edit the article making it better or worst.

Activity 5—Quack Products

It's like your mother used to say: "If it seems too good to be true, it probably is." Yet, thousands of people spend millions of dollars each year on products that claim to hold the cure for their health conditions. When we are desperate, we are more willing to believe questionable claims. Most pharmaceutical companies are in business to make money, investing millions of dollars researching products to cure disease or reduce suffering. If there were a product or substance with potential, they would be the first to use their impressive resources to investigate it. Yet, some unknown advertisers claim to have cures that others don't know. This activity will give you some practice identifying the persuasive techniques most often used by quack promoters.

Directions:

First. Read over the following list of eleven advertising techniques that are often used to promote questionable products or services. They have been identified by the *National Institute on Aging* and *the Federal Trade Commission*.

1. Promise a **quick or painless** cure. For example: *"Shed pounds the natural way without restricting diets or exhausting exercise"*

2. Claim the product is made from a **special, secret, or ancient** formula. For example: *"This product is distilled from the rare Kishiki root, used by Tibetan monks for thousands of years."*

3. Claim to **cure a disease** (such as arthritis or Alzheimer's disease) **that hasn't been cured by medical science.**

4. Make statements that the product is an effective **cure-all** or diagnostic tool for a wide variety of ailments. For example: *"Extremely beneficial in the treatment of arthritis, infections, prostate problems, ulcers, cancer, heart trouble, hardening of the arteries and more."*

---

5. Promote the product using **dramatic words** like "scientific breakthrough," or "miraculous cure." For example: "*A revolutionary innovation formulated by using proven principles of natural health-based medical science.*"

6. Use **impressive-sounding terms.** For example: a weight-loss product describing: *"hunger stimulation point"* and *"thermogenesis."*

7. Use **undocumented case histories** or **personal testimonials** by consumers or doctors claiming amazing results. For example: *"My husband has Alzheimer's disease. He began taking a teaspoonful of this product each day. And now in just 8 days he mowed the grass, cleaned out the garage, weeded the flower beds and we take our morning walk again."*

8. Claim **limited availability** or **advance payment** requirements. For example: *"Hurry. This offer will not last. Send us a check now to reserve your supply."*

9. Promise no-risk **money-back guarantees.** For example: *"If after 30 days you have not lost at least 4 pounds each week, your un-cashed check will be returned to you."*

10. Offer products and services **only by mail** or **from one company.** For example: *"Exclusively available from us."*

11. Offer an additional **free gift** or a **larger amount** of the product as a "special promotion" For example: act now and get an additional 6 oz.

Second. Read the following testimonials found on websites advertising certain products. Use the checklists that follow each testimonial to identify which quackery techniques are being applied.

Third. After completing the checklists, in one page, answer the following questions: **a)** Why do you think people fall for these products? **b)** Should the government do more to control these types of products? **c)** What could you teach family or friends that could help them avoid these types of scams?

Cell-Health Makeover

We have experienced, firsthand, how these 'procaine' based nutriments, which consists of two substances, PABA and DEAE, found naturally in the body, have resulted in noticeable and dramatic health and disease makeovers. From my own father's failing memory which improved after taking the Vitacel products, to a friend's 38 year battle with full blown Psoriasis which miraculously cleared up within 3 months of taking the Vitacel products, and to my own plight with crippling sciatic nerve back pain to which I'd foreseen a pain-filled, medicated future, short of surgery.

The surprise of it all, was, not only did my back pain clear up within 3 weeks, my hair and nails, too, became stronger and healthier, my sleep more restful, my skin more youthful and supple. My arthritic thumb, due to an injury years ago, subsided in discomfort by 75% but when taking an extra vitamin tablet a day, has almost disappeared except for a slight pinch every so often. Also, a wonderful sense of well being enveloped me, no matter what stress or pressure I was facing in life.

Having said all this, these health supplement products, are not intended as a cure, for once a condition has developed, it can return slowly when you stop taking the Vitacel. These products, only available from Cell-Health Makeover, do offer the possibility of halting and reversing aging, health conditions and diseases and in prolonging life.

—Rin Johnson, Vancouver B.C., Canada

Quackery Techniques Checklist										
Secret or Ancient	Quick and/or Painless	Unknown Cure	Cure-all	Dramatic words	Impressive Terms	Case history or Testimonial	Limited Availability	Money-back Guarantees	Exclusively Available	Promotions
Ancient	quick	×	✓	✓	✓	Testimonial	×	×	×	×

Health Care Professionals Testimonials—100% True

"Being in practice for over twenty years and prior to that being a professional athlete, I've always studied nutrition and the thing I've seen most is, remarkable changes (when) we've done detoxing. We see people from all over the world with health care problems and very unusual toxic problems and the results that we're getting with the (liquid Zeolite) are just shocking.

Two leukemia patients came back with their blood results negative, I've had numerous patients with autism where the children are cognitive again and the list just goes on and on. Numerous patients who had the detox and (were) terminal cancer patients with skin cancer they came back negative.

So, it's detoxing the body; it's a nutrient; it's non-toxic and I've never seen anything like it. It's really gotten me jazzed back up in my practice because one of the biggest things we've had to confront is the neurotoxins and the toxins in our environment - It's really been tough for holistic practitioners. So, I feel that this product is something that is just going to change the world.

(When asked how long it takes to see results): It varies from patient to patient. If someone is very toxic, overweight, isn't on the right type of diet, that is going to take a little longer. But, sometimes we'll see it with patients, in the next day."

–Dr. Tom Zorich, D.C., California, USA

Quackery Techniques Checklist										
Secret or Ancient	Quick and/or Painless	Unknown Cure	Cure-all	Dramatic words	Impressive Terms	Case history or Testimonial	Limited Availability	Money-back Guarantees	Exclusively Available	Promotions
Secret	Painless	x	√	√	√	Testimonial	x	x	x	x

Activity 6—Print Ads

To stay in business, magazines and newspapers must have advertising revenue. In fact, many earn more from ads than they do from subscriptions. Some periodicals are very careful not to print deceptive or misleading information, including advertising. Others are less careful. This activity will teach you to recognize and analyze misleading and deceptive print advertisements.

Directions:

1. Acquire a copy of a popular supermarket news or health magazine. These are the ones that are usually placed near the checkout lines. Some examples are: *The National Enquirer, Star, The Globe, National Examiner, Sun, Weekly World News, Radar, ¡Mira!, Shape, Natural Health, Muscle and Fitness, Men's Fitness,* and *Flex.*

2. Thumb through the magazine and identify at least one advertisement for a product, service or book that is intended to affect health in some way.

3. Use the following checklist to identify the questionable techniques and information in the advertisement.

4. Additionally, give examples from the ad that illustrate the questionable technique.

Print Ad Checklist

Magazine/Newspaper name: Architectural Digest

Issue & page number: October 2010 / pg. 61

Is it intended for specific health conditions? Yes

Example: It will take out frown lines between the brows for people between the ages of 18 and 65

Is there an appeal to authority (Dr., scientist, famous, etc?) Yes

Example: Ask the doctor about the product and they will prescribe it when you tell them your medical condition

---

Are there testimonials? Are they believable? Yes

Example: "Proven year after year... with real, noticeable results."

Does it make dramatic or exaggerated claims? No

Example:

Does it provide evidence for claims? No

Example:

Is there any small print? Yes

Example: Important Safety Information

Does it appeal to emotions? (fear/worry, sex, etc.) No

Example:

Does it talk negatively about conventional medicine? (saying it's: dangerous, not natural, mostly about money, etc.) *No*

Example:

Does it claim the treatment is new or secret? *New*

Example: *Botox® Cosmetic is a prescription medicine that is injected into muscles to temporarily treat moderate to severe frown lines between the brows*

Is it generally available or only through one company or site? *Generally*

Example: *Ask the doctor about it and they will prescribe it for you if you tell them about your conditions.*

Does it focus on symptoms that "come and go" naturally? (pain, fatigue, insomnia, etc.) *Yes*

Example: *Temporarily treat frown lines between the brows*

Activity 7—Deceptive Advertising

Some people who promote questionable products or services do so because they truly believe in them. However, some products are marketed by individuals or companies whose primary goal is making many. Many of these marketers are well versed in advertising techniques that have been used for years to persuade people to purchase their products. This activity will help you recognize how these techniques can be used to deceive.

Directions

For this activity you will design a print advertisement intended to convince individuals to send money for your product or service. Imagine your advertisement will appear in a popular supermarket tabloid. You will have one page (8.5 X 11).

Select one condition or health outcome and pair it with one substance or treatment from the following lists to use in your ad:

Condition/Outcome	Product/Treatment
• Obesity • Libido/sex drive • Arthritis • Cancer • Mental clarity or concentration • Skin blemishes or appearance • Overall health, vitality, and energy	• Evergreen sap • A heated belt • Instruction in special postures, posses or movements • Diluted ant venom • Crystallized citrus extracts • Capsules of concentrated ground root from the Andes • An electric device that vibrates at ultra high frequencies

Next, write the text of your add using at least five of the advertising techniques that follow. Be creative with your design and layout.

Techniques Commonly Used in Deceptive Advertising

1. **Appeal to authority** (doctor, scientist, someone famous, etc.)

2. **Appeal to emotions** (fear/worry, sex, self-esteem, etc.)

3. **Small print.**

4. **Talk negatively about conventional medicine** (its: dangerous, not natural, mostly about money, etc.)

5. **Focus on symptoms that "come and go"** naturally (pain, fatigue, insomnia, etc.)

6. Promise a **quick or painless** cure.

7. Claim the product is made from a **special, secret, or ancient** formula.

8. Claim to **cure a disease that hasn't been cured by medical science**.

9. Make statements that the product is an effective **cure-all** or diagnostic tool for a wide variety of ailments.

10. Promote the product using **dramatic words** like "scientific breakthrough," or "miraculous cure."

11. Use **impressive-sounding terms**.

12. Include **undocumented case histories** or **personal testimonials** by consumers or doctors claiming amazing results.

13. Emphasize **limited availability** or **advance payment** requirements.

14. Offer products and services **only by mail** or **from one company**.

15. Offer an additional **free gift** or a **larger amount** of the product as a "special promotion"

Part Two

Conventional
Health Care

Activity 8—**Finding a Good Doctor**

This activity will help you better understand what is important in choosing a good physician.

Directions:

a) Go to the following government websites and read the short advice articles:

- *http://www.ahrq.gov/consumer/cc/cc071508.htm*
- *http://www.nih.gov/news/WordonHealth/apr2003/doctorchoosing.htm*
- *www.opa.ca.gov/healthcare/_downloads/choose-doctor.pdf*

After reading the articles, come up with two additional questions about choosing a doctor and add them to the questionnaires on the following pages.

b) Use the questionnaires on the following pages to interview two adults who have had experience selecting a personal doctor. Have them rate how important each factor is to them and how well their current primary doctors meet each attribute.

c) Use the third worksheet for your personal criteria and rate your current or previous primary doctor (or if you haven't had a personal doctor have a family member rate his or her doctor)

d) In one page, discuss what you learned about others' criteria and your own preferences and what you could do better in the future.

Physician Selection Worksheet 1

Gender ____ Approximate age ____

	How important to you?			How good is your primary doctor?		
	very	some what	not very	very	some what	not very
1. Liked by others I trust						
2. Is specifically male or female						
3. Is covered by my insurance						
4. Years of experience						
5. Wait time to get an appointment						
6. Office wait time						
7. Treats with respect and kindness						
8. Listens and explains things well						
9. -						
10. -						

Comments:

Physician Selection Worksheet 2

Gender ____   Approximate age ____

	How important to you?			How good is your primary doctor?		
	very	some what	not very	very	some what	not very
1. Liked by others I trust						
2. Is specifically male or female						
3. Is covered by my insurance						
4. Years of experience						
5. Wait time to get an appointment						
6. Office wait time						
7. Treats with respect and kindness						
8. Listens and explains things well						
9. -						
10. -						

Comments:

Physician Selection Worksheet (self)

Gender _M_ **Approximate age** _20_

	How important to you?			How good is your primary doctor?		
	very	some what	not very	very	some what	not very
1. Liked by others I trust	✓			✓		
2. Is specifically male or female			✓	✓		
3. Is covered by my insurance	✓			✓		
4. Years of experience	✓			✓		
5. Wait time to get an appointment		✓			✓	
6. Office wait time		✓			✓	
7. Treats with respect and kindness	✓			✓		
8. Listens and explains things well	✓			✓		
9. - E-mail		✓				✓
10. - paper & electronic medical records	✓					✓

Comments:

Activity 9—Being a Good Patient

To have a beneficial relationship with a primary care physician, the patient must also be informed and careful. This activity will help you discover some ways you can enhance your relationship with your doctor.

Directions:

a) For this assignment, you will interview two primary care physicians (i.e., family practice, general practitioner, pediatrician, or gynecologist). In most cases, it would be helpful if your current or past doctor is one of the two interviews (if you don't have a personal doctor, any two doctors willing to talk to you). In-person or telephone interviews are usually most informative, but an exchange by email may also work. Ask the physician for a time that would be most convenient to conduct the interview. Explain that the interview will only take a few minutes and then respect their time during the interview.

b) Record each physician's answers to the questions on the following pages.

c) After, completing the interviews, in one page, discuss what you learned that could help improve interactions with your primary care physician in the future.

Physician Interview 1

To Physician: *Thank you for your time. I have two questions about doctor-patient relations I would like to ask you:*

What are the two most important things patients can <u>*know or believe*</u> that would improve their relationship with their primary care physicians?

1)

2)

What are the two most important things patients can <u>*do*</u> to have a more enjoyable and helpful relationship with their primary care physicians?

1)

2)

Physician Interview 2

To Physician: *Thank you for your time. I have two questions about doctor-patient relations I would like to ask you:*

What are the two most important things patients can <u>*know or believe*</u> that would improve their relationship with their primary care physicians?

1)

2)

What are the 2 most important things patients can <u>*do*</u> to have a more enjoyable and helpful relationship with their primary care physicians?

1)

2)

Activity 9 continued—Being a Good Patient

Activity 10—Mental Health

Often when we talk of health, we limit ourselves to conditions or behaviors that affect the physical body or processes. But, being healthy also includes mental and emotional wellness. Some mental/emotional traits, such as self-esteem, help us to live healthier lives, while others, such as depression, can interfere with having a healthy life. This activity will help you understand the concept of mental health and the ways that professionals can screen for the traits that affect it.

Directions:

This activity will require access to a computer with Internet capabilities. The three most common mental health challenges are depression, anxiety (Generalized Anxiety Disorder (GAD) being the most common), and substance abuse (alcohol being the most common substance).

Enter the following addresses in your internet address bar and read the short, online publications from the National Institutes of Mental Health and of Alcohol Abuse and Alcoholism. They are part of the National Institutes of Health. (If a link does not work, in your web browser type the initials for the institute and the name of the article for example: NIMH "Depression Easy to Read" to locate it)

> Depression…*http://www.nimh.nih.gov/health/publications/depression-easy-to-read/index.shtml*

> Anxiety…_http://www.nimh.nih.gov/health/publications/generalized-anxiety-disorder/index.shtml_

> Alcoholism…_http://pubs.niaaa.nih.gov/publications/RethinkingDrinking/Rethinking_Drinking.pdf_

Next, go to the following internet addresses and personally complete the online mental health screening tools. There are two tests for each disorder. Compare your two scores for each trait (if a particular site is not working, simply skip it). Write your scores for the six tests in the table the follows.

Anxiety

> _http://www.anxietytreatmentnow.com/anxiety_test.html_

> _http://www.healthyplace.com/psychological-tests/gad-test-generalized-anxiety-disorder/_

Depression

> _http://www.depressiontreatmentnow.com/depression_test.html_

> _http://www.healthyplace.com/psychological-tests/goldberg-depression-questionnaire/_

Substance Addiction

➤ *http://www.healthyplace.com/psychological-tests/alcoholism-test/*

➤ *http://www.healthyplace.com/psychological-tests/audit-alcohol-screening-test/*

TEST	SCORE	
Anxiety 1	57.5 / 100	mild – moderate
Anxiety 2	10	
Depression 1	76.25 / 100	severely depressed
Depression 2	43	moderate to severe
Addiction 1	4	
Addiction 2	0	

If you scored moderate or high on any screening tool, don't feel embarrassed to talk to a family member or teacher. Nearly half of all adults will suffer mental health challenges, in one or more of these areas, sometime in their lives. There are many services available including medications, counseling, and other programs, that have proven effective for most people. You could talk to a counselor at your university

---

health or wellness center or visit a private psychiatrist, psychologist, or professional counselor.

You may also want to share this activity with family members or close friends whom you believe may be suffering from one of these common mental health challenges. Encourage them to take the online screenings and read the short articles. They may need your help finding a professional with whom to talk. If you need help locating a therapist visit the National Mental Health Information Center at: *http://mentalhealth.samhsa.gov/publications/allpubs/KEN98-0046/default.asp*

Activity 11—Mental Health Coverage

Insurance plans vary as to the type and amount of mental health services they cover. Through this activity, you will discover what is covered by your insurance plan. (If you do not currently have an insurance plan, either pretend you are on Medicaid or ask a friend about his/her insurance plan.

Directions:

I) Locate the booklet/pamphlet you were given describing your insurance coverage. It should include an *Explanation of Benefits* table or section. It should also have a customer service telephone number you can call for additional information.

II) Using the *Explanation of Benefits* section (and customer service if necessary), complete the table and the questions that follow.

Personal coverage for mental health services				
	# of days allowed	co-pay	deductible	% after deductible met
Inpatient psychiatric care	60	$100	$900	75 %
	# visits allowed per year	co-pay	deductible	% after deductible met
Outpatient psychiatric services	30	$50	$700	55 %
Outpatient alcohol/substance abuse services	7	$25	$1500	80 %
Prescription psychiatric drugs (e.g., antidepressants, antianxiety, etc)		$50	$300	75 %

- What type of counseling services are approved by your insurance? For example, do you have to see a psychiatrist for outpatient counseling or can you see other types of counselors such as psychologists, social workers, or marriage and family therapists?

  I could see other types of counselors that are associated with my family doctor, so that they are approved by my insurance company.

- Do you have to have a referral from your primary care physician to seek psychiatric services?

  Yes, because the primary doctor knows who to choose and recommends a service that is friendly and patient.

III) Once you have completed the preceding table with its accompanying questions, respond to the following scenario:

- Suppose you followed a counselor's recommendations to have weekly counseling sessions for a mental health challenge, what would be your total out of pocket costs for a year? (You will first need to call a local counselor to get their rates)

Activity 12—Dental Care

The primary threat to good dental health is dental plaque. Dental plaque is buildup of mouth bacteria colonies and their waste products. Bacteria feed on the residue of food sugar and starches on teeth. After about 2-3 days, the initial bacteria are displaced by more harmful bacteria that produce acids that can damage tooth enamel and irritate gums. Left unchecked, this can lead to tooth cavities, gingivitis or periodontal disease.

The best way to remove plaque is professional cleaning; that is why you are advised to get your teeth cleaned every 6 months. However, noticeable damage can occur between cleanings if plaque is not addressed. This is the purpose of brushing and flossing—to prevent excessive build up of plaque between cleanings. This activity will help you learn about dental care.

Directions:

A) Before starting this experiment you will need to acquire some items.
- a new toothbrush
- a box of quality dental floss
- a package of dental disclosing tablets. These can usually be purchased for a small price at large drug stores or ordered online (or a dentist may be able to give you some for little or no charge).

- it would also be useful, though not required, to have an angled dental mirror. Again a dentist may be able to assist you in acquiring one. (They can also be purchased online for as little as $2, plus shipping)

This experiment will take at least 5 days. It would work best soon after having your teeth cleaned, but can also be done at other times.

B) First, brush and floss your teeth carefully. Then use a tablet following the instructions. Notice the degree of pink-dyed plaque near the gum line on both your top and bottom teeth. Make a note on the table the follows where you notice the most plaque. Use the chart to identify specific teeth.

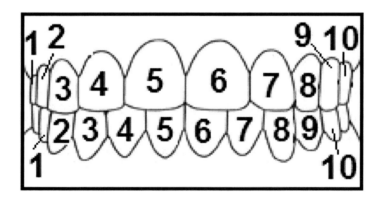

Top row	1	2	3	4	5	6	7	8	9	10
clean										
pink on gum line										
red on gum line										
red on gum line & tooth										
most of tooth pink & red										
Bottom row	1	2	3	4	5	6	7	8	9	10
clean										
pink on gum line										
red on gum line										
red on gum line & tooth										
most of tooth pink & red										

C) Next, brush and floss your top teeth thoroughly for 2 days and ignore your bottom teeth for 2 days. At the end of 2 days, perform the dye test again. Notice if there is a difference in the degree of plaque buildup on the bottom versus the top.

Top row	1	2	3	4	5	6	7	8	9	10
clean										
pink on gum line										
red on gum line										
red on gum line & tooth										
most of tooth pink & red										

Bottom row	1	2	3	4	5	6	7	8	9	10
clean										
pink on gum line										
red on gum line										
red on gum line & tooth										
most of tooth pink & red										

D) For the next 2 days, brush and floss all your teeth carefully twice a day. At the end of 2 days perform the dye test a third time. Notice if you were able to remove some or all the earlier plaque buildup.

Top row	1	2	3	4	5	6	7	8	9	10
clean										
pink on gum line										
red on gum line										
red on gum line & tooth										
most of tooth pink & red										
Bottom row	1	2	3	4	5	6	7	8	9	10
clean										
pink on gum line										
red on gum line										
red on gum line & tooth										
most of tooth pink & red										

During your next visit to the dentist's office, ask the hygienist to explain gingivitis to you. Also, ask which areas of your mouth have the deepest pockets which may need more flossing attention.

Activity 13—Dental Costs

This activity will help you understand how much dental care costs, how much dental insurance costs, and what dental insurance pays for.

Directions:

A) Call two dentists' offices; one should probably be your own dentist. You probably will not need to speak with the dentist; someone in the office should be able to give you the information. If they ask why you want to know, tell them you are working on a project for school. Ask what the full cost (without insurance) is for two common and two less common procedures:

- adult cleaning
- 1-surface metal filling
- single crown
- molar root canal

B) Complete *Dental Table 1*. Write the costs for each procedure in the table and calculate the average cost across the two dental offices for each procedure.

Dental Table 1

PROCEDURES	Full-price for each procedure		Average the 2 dentists' costs
	Dentist 1	Dentist 2	
Adult cleaning	$135	$98	$116.5
1-surface metal filing	$145	$106	$125.5
Single crown	$1,100	$998	$1049
Molar root canal	$900	$1000	$950

C) Next, get online and find two different dental insurance plans. There are many to choose from. Popular plans include Aetna, Careington, Delta, and others. *dentalplans.com* is a good site to compare different plans. Search with your zip code. After the list is populated, click the "Compare All Plans" icon to the right. If *dentalplans.com* is not working, try *dentalinsurance.com* . With this website, choose either a Preferred Provider plan (PPO) or Indemnity plan (patient files for reimbursement)

D) Complete *Dental Table 2*. For the two plans you have selected, look up eight pieces of information and calculate an average cost across the two plans:
- Member fee (individual)
- Yearly deductible
- Waiting period
- Maximum plan will pay in a year
- Your cost for a cleaning
- Your cost for a filling
- Your cost for a crown
- Your cost for a root canal

Dental Table 2

PROCEDURES	Member cost for each procedure		Average the 2 plans' costs
	Plan 1 Aetna	Plan 2 Alliance	
Adult cleaning	$ 55	$ 46	$ 50.5
1-surface metal filling	$ 64	$ 47	$ 55.5
Single crown	$ 593	$ 476	$ 534.5
Molar root canal	$ 574	$ 497	$ 535.5
PLAN DETAILS			
Yearly member fee	$ 104.95	$ 144.95	$ 124.95
Yearly deductible	0	$ 50	$ 25
Plan maximum	0	$ 1500	$ 750
Waiting period	0	6	3

E) Complete *Dental Table 3*. Assume you used the insurance for four years and had eight cleanings, one filing, one crown, and one root canal during this period. What would your total out of pocket cost be with dental insurance versus without dental insurance?

Dental Table 3

	Without insurance	With insurance
Adult cleaning (x8)		
1-surface metal filling		
Single crown		
Molar root canal		
TOTAL PROCEDURE COSTS		
Add deductible (x8)		
Add member fee (x8)		
TOTAL PROCEDURE PLUS OUT OF POCKET COSTS		

Activity 14—Hospitals

Most modern hospitals are staffed by nurses, anesthesiologists, surgeons, physicians, medical assistants and various support staff. Some are on the hospital payroll; others are independent with hospital privileges. Many hospitals are not-for-profit, supported by charities or governments. Others are for-profit, run by insurance companies or healthcare corporations. Hospitals also vary with regard to the physical facilities, equipment and procedures they have available. Some are associated with university medical schools, where new physicians also are trained. Others specialize in certain procedures or services, such as trauma, rehabilitation, psychiatry; or certain clientele, such as children or seniors. The most common model is the *general* or *community* hospital, which serves as the primary health care facility in a region, offering services for a variety of conditions, including emergency and out-patient care. This activity will make you more familiar with your local hospital, the facilities and services it offers, and the typical costs associated with these services.

Directions

First, visit or call your local hospital. If there is more than one, choose the closest that is considered a general purpose hospital. Use the checklists that follow to record which services are available. If there are any you don't recognize, learn about them. For the imaging/testing services, find brief descriptions for each on the Internet.

Then, talk to someone in the billing office; ask about the total costs (before insurance) for the list of common hospital procedures. About 1/3 of all patients using hospitals had one of these top 10 procedures performed. There may also be additional outside fees charged by physicians, but only record the hospital specific fees.

Finally, go to the following *Medicare* website and search for your hospital: *http://www.hospitalcompare.hhs.gov/Hospital/Search/SearchMethod.asp* [Steps: *Search →Criteria →General Search →Check Hospital →Compare →Select All →View Table]*. This will allow you to compare your local hospital to the state and national averages.

Checklist for Hospital Departments

	Alzheimer Care		Open Heart Surgery
	Arthritis Center		Orthopedic Services
	Bariatric/Obesity Services	✓	Out-patient Surgery
	Burn Center		Pain Management Clinic
	Cancer Center		Palliative Care Program
✓	Cardiac Rehabilitation		Patient Education Department
✓	Community Outreach/Education		Pediatric Intensive Care
	Critical Care Ward		Pediatric Ward
	Dialysis Center		Pharmacy
✓	Emergency/Trauma Department	✓	Physical Therapy
	Fertility Clinic		Psychiatric Unit
	Genetic Testing		Pulmonary Disease Center
✓	Heart Center	✓	Radiology Department
	Hospice Care		Respiratory Therapy Department
	Intermediate Nursing Care		Sleep Laboratory
	Labor and Delivery	✓	Speech Therapy Department
	Long-term Care Center		Transplant Services
	Mobile Health Unit		Urgent Care Clinic
	Neonatal Intensive Care		Women's Health Center
	Neurological Services		Wound Care Unit

Checklist for Hospital Imaging and Other Procedures

	PROCEDURE	SHORT DESCRIPTION	MOST COMMON USES
	Angioplasty		
	Angiogram/Arteriogram		
	Barium x-ray		
	Biopsy Pathology		
	Brachytherapy		
	Chemotherapy		
✓	CT Scan	Computed Tomography	obtains images of parts of the body that can't be seen → using standard x-rays
	EBCT		
	ESWL		
	Fluoroscopy		
	Gamma Camera		
	Histopathology Lab		
	IMRT		
	Intravascular Ultrasound		
	IVP		
	MRA		
✓	MRI	Magnetic Resonance Imaging	detects structural abnormalities
	Mammogram		
✓	PET Scan	Positron Emission Tomography	helps to stage and detect certain types of cancer
	Radiation Therapy		
✓	Ultrasound	Device used to examine internal bodily structure	helps to monitor & diagnose conditions in → many parts of the body.
✓	X-ray	form of electromagnetic radiation	used for various diagnostics (dental, orthodontic, medical)

Top Procedures and Imaging Performed in U.S. Hospitals
(Agency of Healthcare Research and Quality, 2003)

Procedure	Percent of Discharges	Fee at local hospital
Blood transfusion	5%	$ 2000
Medical induction, manually assisted delivery, and other procedures to assist delivery	5%	$ 17,000
Respiratory intubation and mechanical ventilation	3%	$ 7,500
Percutaneous coronary angioplasty (PTCA)	2%	$ 15,000
Hemodialysis	2%	$ 1,550

Imaging	Percent of Discharges	Fee at local hospital
Diagnostic cardiac catheterization, coronary arteriography	5%	$ 3,000
Upper gastrointestinal endoscopy, biopsy	3%	$ 1,700
Diagnostic ultrasound of heart (echocardiogram)	2%	$ 2,900
Colonoscopy and biopsy	2%	$ 3,000
CT Scan to detect tumor	1%	$ 1,520

✕ **After completing the worksheets,** in one page, discuss what surprised you most.

Part Three

Complementary and Alternative Medicine (CAM)

Activity 15—CAM Popularity

Does local opinion and experience agree with national trends regarding use of complementary and alternative medicine (CAM)? Find out. With this activity, you will use a short questionnaire to uncover attitude toward CAM therapies, experience with CAM therapies, and reasons for seeking CAM care.

Directions:

First, you will need to design a way to give this survey to a random sample of at least five individuals, who are not relatives.

Then, total your responses across five participants

Next, compare your results with a recent survey by the National Center for Complementary and Alternative Medicine at the U.S. National Institutes of Health:

http://nccam.nih.gov/news/2004/052704.htm

After collecting the surveys and reading the online report, write a one-page summary of your findings, explaining any ways your sample differs from national trends. Attach a summary of your results to your written paper.

CAM Survey

Participant 1		
Gender Male	Age 24	
What is Complementary/Alternative Medicine? Something that will help us feel better without over-the-counter meds.		
Can you think of an example of it? Vitamins		
Have you ever used it? If yes, why? Yes, because each vitamin gives something different & it helps.		
	Ever used	Used last 12 months
Acupuncture	4	2
Ayruvedic	0	0
Homeopathy	0	0
Naturopathy	0	0
Folk medicine	3	1
Chiropractic	5	3
Massage	1	0
Biofeedback	0	0
Meditation	2	1
Deep Breathing	16	3
Hypnosis	1	0
Yoga	0	0
Tai chi	3	2
Qi gong	1	0
Therapeutic tough or reiki	1	0
Special diets	3	1
Megavitamins	12	4
Prayer for health	9	5

Participant 2		
Gender Male	Age 20	
What is Complementary/Alternative Medicine? Activities that help improve the health of people.		
Can you think of an example of it? Sleeping		
Have you ever used it? If yes, why? Yes, because rest helps the body slow down after working a lot.		
	Ever used	Used last 12 months
Acupuncture	1	0
Ayruvedic	1	0
Homeopathy	2	1
Naturopathy	0	0
Folk medicine	1	0
Chiropractic	1	0
Massage	2	0
Biofeedback	0	0
Meditation	0	0
Deep Breathing	3	0
Hypnosis	8	0
Yoga	2	1
Tai chi	6	0
Qi gong	0	0
Therapeutic tough or reiki	2	1
Special diets	1	1
Megavitamins	8	2
Prayer for health	2	1

CAM Survey

Participant 3		
Gender Female	Age 21	
What is Complementary/Alternative Medicine? *Practices that can take the place of medicine.*		
Can you think of an example of it? *Yoga*		
Have you ever used it? If yes, why? *Yes, because exercise could help you be more fit.*		

	Ever used	Used last 12 months
Acupuncture	1	0
Ayruvedic	0	0
Homeopathy	0	0
Naturopathy	0	0
Folk medicine	1	0
Chiropractic	3	0
Massage	6	3
Biofeedback	0	0
Meditation	1	0
Deep Breathing	1	0
Hypnosis	2	0
Yoga	4	2
Tai chi	5	2
Qi gong	1	0
Therapeutic tough or reiki	0	0
Special diets	1	0
Megavitamins	6	4
Prayer for health	1	1

Participant 4		
Gender	Age	
What is Complementary/Alternative Medicine?		
Can you think of an example of it?		
Have you ever used it? If yes, why?		

	Ever used	Used last 12 months
Acupuncture		
Ayruvedic		
Homeopathy		
Naturopathy		
Folk medicine		
Chiropractic		
Massage		
Biofeedback		
Meditation		
Deep Breathing		
Hypnosis		
Yoga		
Tai chi		
Qi gong		
Therapeutic tough or reiki		
Special diets		
Megavitamins		
Prayer for health		

CAM Survey

Participant 5	
Gender	Age
What is Complementary/Alternative Medicine?	
Can you think of an example of it?	
Have you ever used it? If yes, why?	

	Ever used	Used last 12 months
Acupuncture		
Ayruvedic		
Homeopathy		
Naturopathy		
Folk medicine		
Chiropractic		
Massage		
Biofeedback		
Meditation		
Deep Breathing		
Hypnosis		
Yoga		
Tai chi		
Qi gong		
Therapeutic tough or reiki		
Special diets		
Megavitamins		
Prayer for health		

Total of All Participants		
# M 2 # F 1	Ages: 20, 21, 24	
# with accurate definition Three		
# who could think of an example Three		
# who have ever used Three		

	# ever used	# used last 12 months
Acupuncture	6	2
Ayruvedic	1	0
Homeopathy	2	1
Naturopathy	0	0
Folk medicine	5	1
Chiropractic	9	3
Massage	9	3
Biofeedback	0	0
Meditation	3	1
Deep Breathing	20	3
Hypnosis	11	0
Yoga	6	3
Tai chi	14	4
Qi gong	2	0
Therapeutic tough or reiki	3	1
Special diets	5	2
Megavitamins	26	10
Prayer for health	12	7

Activity 16—CAM Research Project

This activity will allow you to develop an in-depth understanding of one alternative health practice. Your instructor may also use this assignment to provide the class with a collection of summaries and resources for several, common alternative health practices.

Your instructor may assign you a topic from the following list. If you are not assigned a specific topic, select something from the list in which you are interested (perhaps the same techniques with which you will use in Activity 18).

Apitherapy	Chiropractic	Iridology	Reflexology
Applied Kinesiology	Colonic Cleansing	Macrobiotics	Tai-Chi/ Chi-Gong
Aromatherapy	Electromagnetic Medicine	Magnet therapy	Therapeutic Touch/Reiki
Ayurvedic Medicine	Feldenkrais Bodywork	Massage as Therapy	Transcendental Meditation
Biofeedback	Homeopathy	Orthomolecular Medicine	Yoga
Biorhythms	Intercessory Prayer	Ozone Therapy	and others

You will become the expert on your topic. The assignment may have two parts if your instructor chooses to assign the 2nd part.

Tai Chi

Directions:

The first part is to prepare a two-page Fact Sheet (one sheet front-&-back). The Fact Sheet should be designed as a resource that can be used as a future reference by the other students in the class. It should be as current as possible. The handout should contain the following parts (for consistency, please use these headings in your handout—please be creative with your color, graphics, layout, etc.):

1. *Overview*: What is it? What is its history? How common is its practice? What is the profile of individuals who usually practice it?
2. *Theory*: What is the theory behind it? Why is believed to work? What health problems are thought to be most responsive to its practice?
3. *Support*: What evidence do practitioners and followers cite to support its practice? (Give references) Also, cite websites and other resources provided by supporters.
4. *Criticism*: Give a citation and brief abstract of a review article from a reputable source criticizing the practice. Also, cite websites and other resources provided by critics.
5. *Recommendations*: Your conclusions—what recommendations and cautions would you give for this practice? What warning signs or *red flags* would you tell interested individuals or groups to watch for?

If assigned, the second part of the assignment is your in-class presentation. This is your chance to discuss interesting information you could not fit on your short handout (please do not make your presentation a duplication of your handout—this is your chance to be creative). Give some anecdotal evidence or specific cases. Ask your instructor how much time you will have for your presentation. Using slides to give your presentation is helpful. Allow a little time for questions and answers at the end of your presentation.

Activity 17—Healthfood Store Visit

Healthfood stores, both locally owned and national chains, are growing with increased popularity of supplements, herbal remedies, muscle builders, and fitness products. This assignment will allow you to determine the level of expertise held by a typical healthfood store worker.

Directions:

You and a partner are to prepare extensively for this assignment—without such preparation, the assignment will not work. In a nutshell, you and a partner are to visit a healthfood store asking about certain symptoms or complaints. Seek advice of the clerks/workers at the store on whether or not a particular product will help with your complaint.

a) Prior to the visit, you will use an internet search engine (such as *Google* or *Yahoo*) to find claims regarding your chosen product (or one assigned by your instructor). For example, if your product were ginseng, you may find stories or product pages that tout the use of ginseng for colds and flu.

b) You will also research what the scientific community is saying about the product. This information may come from governmental web sites (e.g., *NIH*), non-profit medical websites (e.g., *Mayo Clinic, WebMD*), or from articles in professional journals (e.g., *JAMA*, or *New England Journal of Medicine*).

c) Before making your visit, seek approval from your instructor. If you are in a small community, your instructor may need to confirm that students are not all going to the same stores on the same days.

d) Your preparation will give you the ammunition to ask informed questions. When you visit the store, describe to the workers the pretended symptoms you are trying to address or the health-related goal you hope to achieve. Ask them what they would recommend.

If they do not mention your focus product, offer that you have heard rumor the particular product may be helpful. Ask the worker's opinion and advice.

You are not to be confrontational to anyone. You are simply to observe whether they manipulate the truth (often, they don't even realize they are manipulating the truth). Your preparation will help you recognize this.

Your partner is there to make mental notes of information you may miss while engaged in the conversation.

e) If your partner is also a member of class, reverse roles and go to a different healthfood store.

f) After completing the assignment, answer questions on the following page.

Questions about Healthfood Store Visit

1) What store did you visit?

~~CVS / savon Pharmacy~~

Fresh N Easy

2) What day and time do you visit?

Tuesday , 4:30 pm

3) Who did you talk to (what was his/her position at the store)?

The lady that was at the ~~pharmacy~~ counter.
fruit section

4) After explaining your desires, did the worker volunteer that you should try the focus product?

She said to try to drink more water, eat more vegetables, and get more sleep.

5) Describe your conversation with the employee. Did he/she exaggerate the truth? Was he/she well informed? If you had not done the research would you have believed the worker and purchased the product?

a headache?

Lady ~~~~ Pharmacist.

Me: Hi. I was wondering what product I can try to get rid of).
Me: I would try getting more rest.
Me: Well. I had a headache before, but for more than a week.
P: Maybe drinking more water and eating vegetable plus the amount of rest will take the headache away.
Me: What if that didn't help? what kind of product would you think I need?
P: I would say Aleve, but I would try ~~fruit~~ fruits, such as apples, oranges, and bananas. Fruits are another source of Vitamins.

6) What did you learn from this assignment that will affect your attitude toward or practices with regard to healthfood stores?

I learned that fruits is another source of vitamins and nutrients other than the vitamins that give a number of milligrams per pill. Vitamins are expensive, but fruits aren't as expensive.

Healthfood stores tell you what is best to take. Sometimes they would exaggerate as if everything is easy to find when someone would come to the store for the first time and want to know how to get rid of a migrane. Knowing that there is something out there that could also be a source of vitamins and other nutrients that are cheaper than name-brand items that could be able to cure you.

Activity 18—CAM Experiment

This assignment will involve experimenting with complementary/alternative medicine. Think of it as a scientific experiment with only one subject—you.

Directions:

Choose an alternative therapy or practice for which you have been curious. A partial list of alternative health systems and therapies includes:

Apitherapy	Chiropractic	Iridology	Reflexology
Applied Kinesiology	Colonic Cleansing	Macrobiotics	Tai-Chi/ Chi-Gong
Aromatherapy	Electromagnetic Medicine	Magnet therapy	Therapeutic Touch/Reiki
Ayurvedic Medicine	Feldenkrais Bodywork	Massage as Therapy	Transcendental Meditation
Biofeedback	Homeopathy	Orthomolecular Medicine	Yoga
Biorhythms	Intercessory Prayer	Ozone Therapy	and others

Make sure you chose something for which there is potential of noticing some results within 7 days (seek approval from your instructor before beginning).

You may see a therapist or choose a technique or product that involves self administration. The experiment can be done to experience improvement in a specific health condition, general health/vitality, or beauty (skin, hair, etc). DO NOT choose something that will interfere with any current treatment or put you at risk in any way.

Once you have selected the technique, you will take the following steps:

1st.   Develop the methods for your experiment: How will you control for other variables that could affect the condition? How will you be able to measure if it worked? To what will you compare your results?

2nd.   Apply the technique as recommended for at least 7 days.

3rd.   Keep a daily diary of your specific condition or health issue as well as your general health, moods, vitality, etc.

4th.   Write a one-page summary of your methods and the results.

5th.   Write a one-page discussion of your experiment, answering the following questions:

   a) In your opinion, is it valid? Why or why not?
   b) If you were to design a *real* scientific experiment to study this technique, what would it look like?

Activity 19—CAM Insurance

Health insurance is beginning to pay for more and more complementary and alternative care. This activity is to discover the state of affairs where you live, what's available, what it costs, and what insurance will cover.

Directions:

One. Contact local practitioners to learn the cost for one visit for the following procedures:

   a. Chiropractic adjustment for low-back pain

   b. Massage therapy for recurring headaches

   c. Acupuncture for smoking cessation

   d. One additional procedure of your choosing

Two. Learn which of these procedures would be allowed by your current insurance and how much of the cost will be covered by the insurance versus paid by you. (If you currently do not have insurance, pretend you have *Medicare*, or ask a friend about his/her insurance plan).

Three. Find one health insurance policy online that claims to cover alternative therapies and calculate how much it will pay for each of the procedures.

	Local cost for the procedure?	What your insurance covers?	What the online CAM specific plan covers?
Chiropractic adjustment for low-back pain	$55	20%	15%
Massage therapy for recurring headaches	$60	15%	25%
Acupuncture for smoking cessation	$120	30%	20%
Additional procedure of your choosing: Yoga	~~$25~~	~~0%~~	~~5%~~
Hypnosis	$350	25%	20%

Four. Write a one-page summary of your findings, including your opinion of the current state of insurance coverage for complementary and alternative health care.

Part Four

Safety

Activity 20—Home Safety

A large proportion of accidents, injuries, and deaths occur at home. We spend a majority of our time at home, but unlike most public places, no officials inspect our homes or require us to make safety improvements. The most common injuries involve falls, lacerations, burns, and toxic chemicals/substances. In addition to these unintended injuries, some injuries are caused during crimes that can take place on our property. This activity will allow you to assess the safety of your current dwelling.

Directions:

Take a thorough tour of your home, inside and out. While taking your tour, use the following checklist to assess the safety of each feature. If the feature is lacking, decide when and how you will remedy the situation.

After completing the checklist, make a plan to acquire or remedy the safety features that are lacking. Some features will take time or money to fix. Prioritize the order in which you will make the improvements by setting dates to make the changes. Most features you will be able to fix on your own, but some will require you to talk to your landlord or to hire a professional.

	Yes	Safety Feature	Date to be corrected
Indoor	√	Emergency numbers on every phone (e.g., fire, police, ambulance service and poison control).	
	√	House number visible from the street.	
	√	At least one hard-wired telephone for use during power outages.	
	√	Decorative markers on glass doors so people don't walk into them.	
	√	Eliminate clutter, especially on stairs.	
	√	Furnaces, hot water heaters and other gas appliances, as well as chimneys and flues, inspected regularly.	
	√	Ladders: condition and proper use.	
	√	Protective gear (eyes, and ears) when operating power tools or yard equipment.	
	√	Water heater set no higher than 125° to prevent scalding.	
	√	Nonskid strips in bathtubs.	
	√	Grounded circuit breakers on outlets and trip breaks near bathroom and kitchen sinks.	
Outdoor	√	Walkways free of clutter.	
	√	Fence with automatic "child proof" gate around swimming pool.	11-10-10
Fire / Fume	√	Fire extinguishers on every floor and in the kitchen.	
	√	An emergency escape plan and practiced.	11 – 7 - 10
		Fire ladders or stairs for second floor (out only).	11 – 10 - 10
	√	Smoke detectors in every room.	
	√	Carbon monoxide detectors on each floor.	
	√	Radon detectors on each floor.	
	√	Batteries for detectors, replaced twice a year (when you change clocks for Day Light Savings).	
Personal / Crime		Entry door deadbolt and peep hole.	11 – 10 - 10
	√	Pins and wooden rod in sliding glass door.	
	√	Lock on all ground floor windows.	
		Control over access to the building.	11 - 10 - 10
		24-hour lighting of premises.	11 – 10 – 10
	√	Mailboxes and laundry rooms in well lit areas.	
	√	Complex tenant crime watch.	

Activity 21—First Aid

Most people have first aid kits in their homes, but don't give them much thought after they initially acquire them. Only when they need them, do they discover that something important is missing or is somewhere in the house they can't find. Many of the pre-packaged kits sold in stores contain primarily bandages and a few generic ointments, but not everything needed for other emergencies. Oftentimes, it is cheaper to make a kit from scratch and it will contain more items than pre-packaged kits. Making a kit from scratch or supplementing a current kit will also give you a better idea of what supplies will be available in a time of emergency. This activity will provide this opportunity.

Directions

Many lists for First-Aid kits are available. Although they may disagree in some ways, they agree on most items. The checklist included in this activity is a comprehensive list compiled from several sources including the Federal *ready.gov* website.

✓ Gather all the emergency supplies in your home to the kitchen table. Check off all the items you have on the checklist. Make a plan to acquire items you are lacking.

✓ In addition to having an adequately stocked kit, first-aid requires knowledge of how to respond in an emergency. Find a first-aid course in your area. A course is likely offered on your campus, perhaps through your wellness center, student center, or an academic department. You can also check *redcross.org* for a course in your area. There are two types of courses: 1) lifesaving courses that only focus on emergencies that could result in immediate death (breathing, heart stopping, excessive bleeding) and 2) more comprehensive courses that teach how to deal with other issues such as burns, breaks, poisoning, contusions, etc.). At minimum, make a plan to take a basic lifesaving course.

Yes	Item	Date to be corrected
√	Container that can be locked or childproofed	
√	First-aid manual	
Home health equipment:		
	"baby bulb" suction device	12 - 2010
√	Cotton balls	
√	Cotton swabs	
	Face mask for CPR	1 - 2011
√	Heat pack, instant disposable	
√	Ice pack, instant disposable	
√	Gloves, latex and non-latex	
√	Hand sanitizer	
√	Hot-water bottle	
√	Matches	
√	Measuring spoon, cup or syringe for medicine	
√	Meat tenderizer (for insect bites)	
	Moleskin	1 - 2011
√	Needles	
√	Paper & pencil	
√	Paper drinking cups	
√	Safety pins	
√	Save-A-Tooth storage device	
√	Scissors	
√	Small flashlight	
√	Soap	
√	Space blanket	
√	Thermometer	
√	Tongue blades	
√	Tweezers, to remove ticks and small splinters	

Yes	Item	Date to be corrected
Medicine for emergencies:		
√	Activated Charcoal (for poisoning emergencies)	1 - 2011
√	Antacid	
√	Antibiotic ointment, such as bacitracin, polysporin	
√	Antiseptic wipes, alcohol, or povidone-iodine	
√	Burn ointment to prevent infections	
	Calamine lotion for stings or poison ivy	11 - 10 - 2010
√	Diarrhea medication	
√	Eyewash (such as contact lens saline solution)	
	Hydrocortisone cream or ointment for itching	12 - 2010
√	Hydrogen Peroxide	
√	Oil of Cloves (for tooth ache)	
√	Pain medication (aspirin, acetaminophen)	
√	Sugar or glucose solution	
√	Syrup of Ipecac (to induce vomiting)	
Medicine for sickness:		
√	Antihistamine	
V	Decongestant	
√	Expectorant	
√	Prescription medications needed regularly (e.g., insulin, blood pressure, heart, inhaler)	
Bandages and dressings:		
√	Adhesive bandages (e.g., Band-Aid); assorted sizes	
√	Aluminum finger splints	
√	Elastic (ACE) bandage for wrapping joint injuries	
√	Eye shield, pads, and bandages	
√	Gauze pads	
√	Latex or non-latex gloves to reduce contamination risk	
√	Tape, waterproof hypoallergenic	
√	Triangular bandage for wrapping making an arm sling	

Activity 21 continued—First Aid

Activity 22—Emergencies

Sometimes the greatest threat of injury or death is not due to personal lifestyle of behaviors, but to disasters. Although we cannot prevent or usually even predict most disasters, we can be prepared to respond quickly once they have occurred. Preparation includes knowing how to respond to different emergencies, having a personal and/or family plan in place ahead of time, and having an emergency kit in case you need to flee your home or even the city. This activity will allow you to assess your preparedness and make plans to be better prepared.

Directions:

The type of disasters for which you should prepare depends on both the natural and built environments in which you live. Potential emergencies can include:

Natural	Human Caused
Cold, extreme	Biological Threat
Earthquakes	Blackouts
Floods	Chemical Threat
Heat, extreme	Explosions
Hurricanes	Fires
Landslide (often human caused)	Nuclear Threat
Tornadoes	Radiation Threat
Tsunamis	
Volcanoes	
Wildfires (often human caused)	

a) Go to the following website to learn which threats are most common in your area: *http://www.ready.gov/america/local/index.html*

b) Visit the following website and test your personal emergency preparedness: *http://www.whatsyourrq.org/form.php*

c) The Federal Emergency Management Agency has a consumer-focused website to help citizens better understand and prepare for emergencies. This website includes a short video outlining the basic steps to emergency preparedness. Watch the video; you will need to have *flash* capabilities on your computer to watch it: *http://www.ready.gov/america/about/_flash/movie15.html*

d) There are several lists for emergency kits available. In general, you will need food, water, protection from the elements, personal supplies, documents, money, and various types of equipment. What follows is a compilation of more than one list including the checklist on *ready.gov*. Identify a container in which to keep your kit. Check off the items you already have as you place them in your kit. Make plans to acquire or improvise the items you are lacking.

e) Complete the emergency plan form and give copies to family and close friends.

3-Day Emergency Evacuation Kit

Yes	Item	Date to be corrected
Food and Water		
	Water, 1 gallon per person per day, for 3 days (for drinking and sanitation)	
	Portable water filter OR chlorine bleach and medicine dropper – in an emergency ,make potable water by adding 16 drops of bleach per gallon (never use scented, color safe or bleaches with added cleaners).	
	Food, 3-day supply of non-perishable, dried or canned.	
	Can opener for food (if kit contains canned food)	
	Mess kits (or paper cups, plates and plastic utensils)	
Bedding, Clothing and Shelter		
	Change of clothing including undergarments, socks, long sleeved shirt, long pants and sturdy shoes (warm outerwear if you live in a cold-weather climate).	
	Rain gear or poncho	
	Sheet and sleeping bag (or warm blanket) for each person.	
	Space blanket	
	Small tent (or plastic sheeting and duct tape) to shelter-in-place	
Personal Supplies		
	Sanitation items (moist wipes, toilet tissue, garbage bags, soap, hand sanitizer, etc)	
	Toiletries in waterproof bag (feminine hygiene, tooth care, comb, etc.)	
	Infant formula and diapers (if applicable)	
	Pet food and extra water for your pet (if applicable)	
	Prescription glasses and medication (if applicable)	

Yes	Item	Date to be corrected
Equipment		
	First aid kit (see Activity 21)	
	Battery-powered or hand crank radio with weather radio	
	Flashlight	
	Extra batteries for radio and flashlight	
	Whistle to signal for help	
	Dust mask per person, to help filter contaminated air	
	Wrench or pliers or super tool to turn off utilities	
	Cell phone with chargers	
	Matches in a waterproof container or lighter	
	Local maps	
	Paper and pencil	
	Pocket Knife	
	Candles (helpful but not required)	
	Flares (helpful but not required)	
	Shovel, axe, rope (helpful but not required)	
	Fire Extinguisher (helpful but not required)	
	Books, games, or children's activities (helpful but not required)	
Personal Documents (in a water-proof container!)		
	First aid and/or emergency response books	
	Cash or traveler's checks and credit cards	
	Pre-Paid Phone Cards	
	Copies of important documents (such as Birth/Marriage, Wills, Passports, Contracts, Insurance, bank account, and immunization records, and perhaps family photos and history)	
Miscellaneous		
	Container for kit items (duffel bags or back packs, work great). Make sure you can lift/carry it!	

Ready.Gov   Family Emergency Plan

Before an emergency happens, sit down as a family and decide how you will get in contact with each other, where you will go and what you will do in an emergency. Keep a copy of this plan in your emergency supply kit or another safe place where you can access it in the event of a disaster.

Out-of-Town Contact Name:	
Email:	Telephone Number:
Neighborhood Meeting Place:	Telephone Number:
Regional Meeting Place:	Telephone Number:
Evacuation Location:	Telephone Number:

Fill out the following information for each family member and keep it up to date.

Name:	Social Security Number:
Date of Birth:	Important Medical Information:
Name:	Social Security Number:
Date of Birth:	Important Medical Information:
Name:	Social Security Number:
Date of Birth:	Important Medical Information:
Name:	Social Security Number:
Date of Birth:	Important Medical Information:
Name:	Social Security Number:
Date of Birth:	Important Medical Information:
Name:	Social Security Number:
Date of Birth:	Important Medical Information:

Write down where your family spends the most time: work, school and other places you frequent. Schools, daycare providers, workplaces and apartment buildings should all have site-specific emergency plans that you and your family need to know about.

Work Location 1	School Location 1
Address:	Address:
Phone Number:	Phone Number:
Evacuation Location:	Evacuation Location:
Work Location 2	School Location 2
Address:	Address:
Phone Number:	Phone Number:
Evacuation Location:	Evacuation Location:

Important Information	Name	Telephone #	Policy #
Doctor(s):			
GP:			
Other:			
Other:			
Other:			
Pharmacist:			
Medical Insurance:			
Homeowners/Rental Insurance:			
Veterinarian / Kennel(for pets):			

Part Five

Diet and Nutrition

Activity 23—Diet Analysis

Often, we think we are eating a fairly healthy diet until we take the time to examine it closely. This activity will give you an opportunity to monitor your eating and analyze whether your typical dietary practices are healthy or unhealthy.

Directions:

1st. Using the worksheets provided, record everything you eat for 7 days. Choose a week that represents a typical week for you. You may find it helpful to copy the following pages and carry them in your pocket throughout the day.

2nd. Review what you ate for the last 7 days; then, rate your eating for each of the statements on the *Diet Quality Analysis* tool.

3rd. Compare your total score with the scoring rubric. Review the items suggested in the rubric.

4th. Write a one-page analysis of your typical diet. Discuss changes you could make to improve your diet in the future.

Day 1	Breakfast	Slice of bread ham and cheese
	Snack	Granola Bar
	Lunch	Rize Chicken
	Snack	
	Supper	Rize Fried chicken vegetable soup
	Snack	

Day 2	Breakfast	Slice of Bread ham ad cheese
	Snack	Granola Bar
	Lunch	Noodle Rice Chicken
	Snack	
	Supper	Rice Beef w/ chili Broccoli
	Snack	

Day 3	Breakfast	Bagel ham and geese
	Snack	Granola Bar
	Lunch	Rice Pork Lettuce & tomatoes
	Snack	
	Supper	Broccoli Rice chicken
	Snack	

Day 4	Breakfast	
	Snack	
	Lunch	
	Snack	
	Supper	
	Snack	

Day 5	Breakfast	
	Snack	
	Lunch	
	Snack	
	Supper	
	Snack	

Day 6	Breakfast	
	Snack	
	Lunch	
	Snack	
	Supper	
	Snack	

Day 7	Breakfast	
	Snack	
	Lunch	
	Snack	
	Supper	
	Snack	

DIET QUALITY ANALYSIS

In the spaces provided, write the number that most represents your typical eating.

0 = never   1 = rarely   2 = occasionally   3 = sometimes   4 = often   5 = consistently

3   When I have a snack between meals, I choose healthy foods.

4   My diet is low in fat (*I usually avoid fried food, processed meat, frozen meals, ice-cream, cheese, margarine, red meat and snack foods*).

3   My sodium intake is reasonable (*I limit the amount of boxed or canned foods in my diet and rarely add table salt*).

4   I avoid fast food restaurants.

4   I start each day with a healthy breakfast.

5   I avoid caffeine.

4   I limit my consumption of refined sugar (*candy, soft drinks, sugary cereal, pastries, cookies etc.*).

4   I usually eat only when I'm hungry.

3   I try to spread my eating across the day (3+ *meals & snacks*).

5   I drink plenty of water (*6 drinks or more a day*).

3   I eat five servings of fruits and veggies a day.

4   I eat a wide variety of plant foods (*not always the same ones*).

4   I try to eat mostly whole grains and minimally-processed foods

50   **TOTAL**

Diet Analysis Scoring Rubric

56-65   **EXCELLENT**: You're doing a great deal to promote your health through good nutrition

46-55   **GOOD**: You're doing better than most. You might want to look at individual habits for which you scored less than 4.

36-45   **SO-SO**: You eat like many Americans, but can do better. Start with those items less than 3.

26-35   **POOR**: It's time to take a closer look at your eating and how it can affect your health. Focus on those items 2 or less.

<26   **LOOK OUT**: Your eating patterns are unhealthy. Now is the time to make some changes.

Activity 24—Food Labels

Food labels help us determine how much food we should eat and the nutritional quality of the food we do eat. In the United States, we get too much of some nutrients and too little of others. Nutrition in food can be considered in two general groups: macro and micro nutrients.

As the name implies, macro nutrients are present in foods in large quantities. The three types of macro nutrients are proteins, fats, and carbohydrates. Carbohydrates are the body's preferred fuel source. Many Americans get too little fiber and too many simple carbohydrates (sugar), which increases risk for diabetes. Fat is the body's backup energy source, but many Americans get too much fat (particularly saturated and trans fats) and cholesterol, which increase risk for heart disease.

Micro nutrients are present in foods in much smaller quantities. The two primary groups are vitamins and minerals. Important vitamins include Vitamin A and Vitamin C. Common minerals many Americans lack include Calcium and Iron; many Americans get too much Sodium. This activity will help you learn ways to use food labels to make the most of your diet.

Directions

1) Go to the U.S. Department of Agricultural website "MyPyramid." *http://www.mypyramid.gov/mypyramid/index.aspx.* Enter your personal data to calculate the number of calories you should consume per day.

$$\frac{2800}{2000} = 1.4$$

2) Divide your recommended calories by 2000 to get your "Nutrition Data" multiplier. For example, if you are supposed to eat 2300 calories, then *your multiplier* is 1.15; for 1800 calories, the multiplier would be 0.90.

3) Retrieve the original packages for three foods you eat regularly. In the middle column, customize the *% Daily Values* by multiplying by *your multiplier* number. Also, divide the *Calories* by the number of calories you are supposed to eat to make them percentages and write the % in the middle column.

4) Compare each *% Daily Value* to the % for total calories. If the percentages are nearly the same, the food is average for that nutrient. Nutrients for which we should limit our intake include: *Total Fat, Saturated Fat, Cholesterol* and *Sodium*. Nutrients for which most people need more include: *Dietary Fiber, Vitamin A, Vitamin C, Calcium,* and *Iron*. Decide whether the food is *much better than average, better than average, average, worse than average* or *much worse than average*. For example a nutrient % that is twice the Calories % is *much better* or *much worse* than average depending on the nutrient.

5) After completing the worksheets, in one page, discuss a) what you found, b) what surprised you, and c) what changes, if any, you will make.

Food 1:

Nutrition Facts Serving Size Serving Per Container	**% Daily Value**	**Much better than average**	**Better than average**	**Average**	**Worse than average**	**Much worse than average**
Calories						
Total Fat						
Saturated Fat						
Trans Fat						
Cholesterol						
Sodium						
Total Carbohydrate						
Dietary Fiber						
Sugars						
Protein						
Vitamin A						
Vitamin C						
Calcium						
Iron						

Food 2:						
Nutrition Facts Serving Size Serving Per Container	**% Daily Value**	Much better than average	Better than average	Average	Worse than average	Much worse than average
Calories						
Total Fat						
Saturated Fat						
Trans Fat						
Cholesterol						
Sodium						
Total Carbohydrate						
Dietary Fiber						
Sugars						
Protein						
Vitamin A						
Vitamin C						
Calcium						
Iron						

Food 3: **Nutrition Facts** Serving Size Serving Per Container	% Daily Value	Much better than average	Better than average	Average	Worse than average	Much worse than average
Calories						
Total Fat						
Saturated Fat						
Trans Fat						
Cholesterol						
Sodium						
Total Carbohydrate						
Dietary Fiber						
Sugars						
Protein						
Vitamin A						
Vitamin C						
Calcium						
Iron						

Activity 25—Fastfood Nutrition

This assignment will help you discover whether the food served at your favorite restaurants is nutritious and healthy.

Directions:

I.   From the following list, select two fast-food restaurants that you frequent most.

   Arby's, Burger King, Chick-fil-A, Dairy Queen, Hardies, KFC, Long John Silvers, McDonalds, PizzaHut, Subway, Taco Bell, Wendy's Chipotle

II. Use the Internet to look up nutrition data for each restaurant. For example, in the *Google* or *Yahoo* search bar type a phrase such as "KFC nutrition." Look for addresses that are associated with the official company website.

III. Using the data provided online, construct a 'typical' meal that totals approximately 1300 calories; one for each restaurant.

IV. Fill in the tables with the nutrient values or percents (%) as indicated above each column. These are not all the nutrients of concern, but simply a selection of some of the important nutrients. If a particular nutrient is not listed, simply skip it. Total the amounts for each column.

V.   Compare the typical meals from the two restaurants with the example home-cooked meal and answer the questions at the end.

Fastfood Restaurant 1 ___Chipotle___

	cal	g	mg	mg	g	g	% DV	% DV	% DV	% DV
ITEMS	Cal	Fat	Chol.	Sodium	Fiber	Protein	Vit A	Vit C	Calcium	Iron
EX: Mystery Burger Deluxe	510cal	28g	70mg	550mg	2g	32g	2%	1%	4%	8%
Flour tortilla	290	9	0	670	2	7	0	0	20	15
Steak	190	6.5	65	320	0	30	2	0	2	15
Pinto beans	120	1	5	530	10	7	2	2	4	10
Corn salsa	80	1.5	0	410	3	3	4	10	0	4
Fajita Vegetables	20	0.5	0	170	1	1	4	30	2	2
chips	570	27	0	420	8	8	0	2	4	6
TOTALS	1270	45.5	70	2320	24	56	12	44	32	52

Fastfood Restaurant 2 ___Subway___

	cal	g	mg	mg	g	g	% DV	% DV	% DV	% DV
ITEMS	Cal	Fat	Chol.	Sodium	Fiber	Protein	Vit A	Vit C	Calcium	Iron
EX: Mystery Burger Deluxe	510cal	28g	70mg	550mg	2g	32g	2%	1%	4%	8%
6" Meatball Marinara	580	23	45	1530	9	24	40	45	20	25
6" Chicken & Bacon Ranch	570	28	95	1190	5	35	15	25	25	20
TOTALS	1150	51	140	2720	14	59	55	70	45	45

Home-cooked meal example

ITEMS	Cal (cal)	Fat (g)	Chol. (mg)	Sodium (mg)	Fiber (g)	Protein (g)	Vit A (% DV)	Vit C (% DV)	Calcium (% DV)	Iron (% DV)
chicken breast (1 med.)	284	6	146	128	0	54	0	0	2%	10%
Spaghetti (1 cup)	220	1	0	183	3	8	0	0	1%	10%
spaghetti sauce (½ cup)	112	3	0	527	4	2	20%	5%	3%	5%
corn (1 cup)	130	2	3	402	4	4	6%	10%	0	4%
green beans (1 cup)	34	0	0	331	4	3	15%	9%	6%	5%
Cantaloupe (half)	95	0	0	44	3	3	187%	169%	3%	3%
Green salad (v. large)	15	0	0	28	2	3	138%	33%	5%	8%
lite dressing (3 tbsp)	84	9	0	597	0	0	0	0	0	0
Brownies (2 small)	224	14	36	169	0	2	8%	0	2%	6%
TOTALS	1198	35	185	2404	22	79	374%	226%	22%	49%

Questions

1) Where did most of the fat come from in each of meal?

The chips from chipotle

6" Chicken & Bacon Ranch from Subway

Questions cont.

2) Where did most of the cholesterol come from in each meal?

The steak from Subway and the Chicken & Bacon Ranch sandwich from Chipotle

3) Where did most of the fiber come from in each meal?

Pinto beans from Chipotle.
6" Meatball Marinara from Subway

4) What surprised you most about each meal?

Subway: The Chicken & Bacon Ranch sandwich has a higher cholesterol amount than the Meatball marinara sandwich.

Chipotle: The chips gives more fat than the steak burrito.

5) Why do you think many people would choose one of the fast-food meals over the home-cooked meal?

Many people choose to have a fast-food meal over a home-cooked meal because they might want to have something different than food that they eat at home every day.

6) If you decided to eat at these fast-food restaurants, what could be done to make these meals healthier?

I would ask them to add more vegetables if the meal came with it.

7) What could these fast-food restaurants do to allow healthier selections?

They should provide more kinds of salads and vegetables to choose from to allow a healthier selection.

Activity 26—Superfoods

Sometimes we hear rumors about Superfoods, foods that are unusually high in nutrition, for instance wheatgrass juice and spirulina, a type of seaweed. In reality, there are no "Superfoods." But, there are foods that are higher in nutrition relative to others. This activity will help you identify some of these high-nutrition foods.

Directions:

1. For this activity you will be using an online tool called *NutritionData (ND)*. It's free to use, but you may need to register to access some of the screens.

   - In your Internet address box type: *www.nutritiondata.com*.
   - Go to *Tools* and click on the **Nutritional Target Map Search**.
   - Under the heading **Related Search Results**, click on the link to **Better choices for optimal health**.
   - Select a food category (for example, *Cereal Grains and Pasta*)
   - Select a food with a high **ND rating**. Choose foods that you recognize and would consider eating.

2. Find one "high-nutrition" food for each of the following seven categories: a) grain, pasta, or breakfast cereal; b) vegetable; c) fruit; d) nut or legume; e) meat (fish, poultry, beef, or pork); f) diary or egg; g) snack. You may need to preview a few foods in each category to find the best. For ease of comparison, set each food serving size to 1 ounce.

3. In the report that is generated for each food, "high-nutrition" will be judged by five factors: a) *ND Rating*, b) *Fullness Factor*, c) *Glycemic Load*, d) *Inflammation Factor*, e) *Completeness Score*. Write the score for each food under the appropriate factors in the table.

Consumer Health Activities

4. While on the *NutritionData* website, read the definitions for the various factors, by clicking on the questions marks "?" next to each factor.

5. Go to a grocery store, or call around, to find out the cost of each food; then calculate the *cost per ounce* for each food.

6. Compare the foods you have identified with two oft-rumored superfoods: wheatgrass juice and spirulina.

7. When you have finished 1-6, answer the questions about your findings.

	Specific Food	ND Rating	Fullness Factor	Glycemic Load	Inflammation Factor	Completeness Score	Cost per ounce
grain, pasta or cereal	Spaghetti, spinach cooked	3.1	2.2	4	-24	36	$0.07
vegetable	Broccoli, cooked	5	4.4	0	39	93	$1.67
fruit	Bananas, raw	2.8	2.5	2	-14	42	$0.10
nut or legume	Soybeans, raw	4.3	2.5	3	-6	63	$0.12
meat	Chicken, fryers, broilers or giblets, cooked simmered	4	3.1	0	-51	69	$0.20
dairy or egg	Yogurt, vanilla & lemon nonfat milk low-calorie	2.7	3.6	1	-8	47	$0.05
snack	Formulated bar, Masterfood USA	4.2	2.3	11	n/a	76	$0.12
Jamba Juice: wheatgrass		2.7	4.5	1	n/a	25	0.19
seaweed: spirulina		4.1	2.9	3	-10	69	1.50

Consumer Health Activities

Questions

One. In your opinion, do some foods deserve to be called superfoods, why or why not?

Two. Is it expensive to get high nutrition? Give examples.

Three. Individuals with what type of health conditions or lifestyles should pay most attention to each of the 5 nutrition health measures?

ND Rating	
Fullness Factor	
Glycemic Load	
Inflammation Factor	
Completeness Score	

Questions cont.

Four.   If someone wanted to eat high-level nutrition without continuously
looking up foods, are there similarities or patterns among these high-
nutrition foods that could help them select high-nutrition foods? What
advice would you give?

Five.   Based on what you have learned, how could you realistically make your
diet more nutritious?

Activity 27—Nutrition Messages on TV

Recently, there has been increased focus on the culture surrounding food in this country and the way the media and advertisers portray food. They assignment will allow you a look into a small window of the popular culture surrounding food.

Directions:

For this assignment, you will watch 2 hours of broadcast television and analyze the amounts and types of messages that are related to food. Limit yourself to the following channels: ABC, CBS, FOX, and NBC.

I.   Select a target audience, either general adult or child. For general adults, you will watch between 8 pm and 11 pm on a Weekday evening. For children, you will watch between 7 am and noon on a Saturday morning (select channels with children's' programming).

II. While you watch, use the worksheet on the following page to record food messages. Enjoy the programs, but don't get so involved that you miss subtle food messages. Pay attention not only to the words, but the implied meanings. Look for messages in commercials as well as the entertainment shows.

III. After completing the worksheet for 2 hours of programming, answer the questions at the end.

TV Nutrition Messages Worksheet

Time	Channel	Program	Character (or company if a commercial)
	Summary of message:		

Time	Channel	Program	Character (or company if a commercial)
	Summary of message:		

Time	Channel	Program	Character (or company if a commercial)
	Summary of message:		

Time	Channel	Program	Character (or company if a commercial)
	Summary of message:		

Time	Channel	Program	Character (or company if a commercial)
	Summary of message:		

Time	Channel	Program	Character (or company if a commercial)
	Summary of message:		

TV Nutrition Messages Worksheet

Time	Channel	Program	Character (or company if a commercial)
Summary of message:			
Time	Channel	Program	Character (or company if a commercial)
Summary of message:			
Time	Channel	Program	Character (or company if a commercial)
Summary of message:			
Time	Channel	Program	Character (or company if a commercial)
Summary of message:			
Time	Channel	Program	Character (or company if a commercial)
Summary of message:			
Time	Channel	Program	Character (or company if a commercial)
Summary of message:			

TV Nutrition Messages Worksheet

Time	Channel	Program	Character (or company if a commercial)
	Summary of message:		
Time	Channel	Program	Character (or company if a commercial)
	Summary of message:		
Time	Channel	Program	Character (or company if a commercial)
	Summary of message:		
Time	Channel	Program	Character (or company if a commercial)
	Summary of message:		
Time	Channel	Program	Character (or company if a commercial)
	Summary of message:		
Time	Channel	Program	Character (or company if a commercial)
	Summary of message:		

TV Nutrition Messages Worksheet

Time	Channel	Program	Character (or company if a commercial)

Summary of message:

Time	Channel	Program	Character (or company if a commercial)

Summary of message:

Time	Channel	Program	Character (or company if a commercial)

Summary of message:

Time	Channel	Program	Character (or company if a commercial)

Summary of message:

Time	Channel	Program	Character (or company if a commercial)

Summary of message:

Time	Channel	Program	Character (or company if a commercial)

Summary of message:

Questions

1) Did anything surprise you?

2) How many food messages were given?

3) What were the dominant messages?

4) What were the implied messages?

5) If the target audience believed and followed the messages what would be the results?

6) What advice would you give to television viewers or parents of child viewers?

7) Should there be changes in what is allowed to be presented regarding food? If yes, what?

Part Six

Fitness and
Weight Management

Activity 28—Body Weight

We have been hearing a lot lately about the health risks of being overweight. In reality, the risks depend on the degree a person is overweight. Evidence seems to suggest that those who are slightly overweight are at about the same health risk as those at a normal (recommended) weight and may actually face somewhat lower risk for some diseases than those who are underweight. It is the very overweight, described by the word "obese," that face the greatest health risk.

The generally accepted measure of obesity is the Body Mass Index (BMI). Though it is mostly accurate, in some circumstances it may overestimate body fat in athletes and others who have a muscular build, and underestimate body fat in older persons and others who have lost muscle mass.

Directions:

1. Use the table, *BMI Calculated from Height and Weight* that follows to determine your BMI based on your height and weight. If your height or weight is not included, use the online calculator listed under the table.

2. In determining health risk, it's important to examine not only total body fat, but the distribution of fat in the body. Those with fat primarily in the abdominal area are at greater risk. Abdominal fat is approximated by waist circumference.

   Determine your waist circumference by placing a measuring tape snugly around your waist. Disease risk increases with a waist measurement of over 40 inches in men and over 35 inches in women.

3. Use the table, *Risks of Obesity-Associated Diseases by BMI and Waist Circumference*; to get an idea of whether your BMI combined with your waist circumference increases your risk for developing obesity associated diseases or conditions.

---

4. In addition to being overweight and carrying abdominal fat, there are additional risk factors that can increase your chance of developing hypertension, type 2 diabetes, heart disease, stroke, and certain cancers. Look over the list below and determine if you have any of these other risk factors:

- high blood pressure (hypertension)
- high LDL-cholesterol ("bad" cholesterol)
- low HDL-cholesterol ("good" cholesterol)
- high triglycerides
- high blood glucose (sugar)
- family history of premature heart disease
- physical inactivity
- cigarette smoking
- high levels of stress

5. For those considered obese (or those who are overweight plus have two or more additional risk factors), weight loss is recommended. Even a modest weight loss (10 percent of your current weight) could help to lower your risk of developing obesity-related diseases. If you are at risk, make an appointment with your primary care physician to discuss your options. You will also want to set goals to lower your weight or body fat.

   If you are overweight, but do not have a high waist measurement or other risk factors, rather than weight loss, your goal should be to prevent further weight gain.

6. Though not required, it would be helpful to go through the same process with loved ones, who you suspect may be at risk.

1) BMI = 23
2) Normal

BMI Calculated from Height and Weight													
BMI	**19**	**20**	**21**	**22**	**23**	**24**	**25**	**26**	**27**	**28**	**29**	**30**	**35**
Height (inches)	Weight (pounds)												
58	91	96	100	105	110	115	119	124	129	134	138	143	167
59	94	99	104	109	114	119	124	128	133	138	143	148	173
60	97	102	107	112	118	123	128	133	138	143	148	153	179
61	100	106	111	116	122	127	132	137	143	148	153	158	185
62	104	109	115	120	126	131	136	142	147	153	158	164	191
63	107	113	118	124	130	135	141	146	152	158	163	169	197
64	110	116	122	128	134	140	145	151	157	163	169	174	204
65	114	120	126	132	138	144	150	156	162	168	174	180	210
66	118	124	130	136	142	148	155	161	167	173	179	186	216
67	121	127	134	140	146	153	159	166	172	178	185	191	223
68	125	131	138	144	151	158	164	171	177	184	190	197	230
69	128	135	142	149	155	162	169	176	182	189	196	203	236
70	132	139	146	153	160	167	174	181	188	195	202	209	243
71	136	143	150	157	165	172	179	186	193	200	208	215	250
72	140	147	154	162	169	177	184	191	199	206	213	221	258
73	144	151	159	166	174	182	189	197	204	212	219	227	265
74	148	155	163	171	179	186	194	202	210	218	225	233	272
75	152	160	168	176	184	192	200	208	216	224	232	240	279
76	156	164	172	180	189	197	205	213	221	230	238	246	287

If your weight, height, or BMI is not listed on the table, you can use the online calculator from the National Heart Lund and Blood Institute to calculate your BMI: *http://www.nhlbisupport.com/bmi/*

Classification of Overweight and Obesity by BMI, Waist Circumference, and Associated Disease Risks

	BMI (kg/m^2)	Obesity Class	Disease Risk* compared to Normal Weight and Waist Circumference	
			Men 40 in or less Women 35 in or less	Men > 40 in Women > 35 in
Underweight	< 18.5		-	-
Normal	18.5 - 24.9		-	-
Overweight	25.0 - 29.9		Increased	High
Obesity	30.0 - 34.9	I	High	Very High
	35.0 - 39.9	II	Very High	Very High
Extreme Obesity	40.0 +	III	Extremely High	Extremely High

* Disease risk for type 2 diabetes, hypertension, and CVD.

National Heart Lund and Blood Institute

Activity 29—Popular Diets

When it comes to diets, there are the tried-and-true, the trends, and the fads. Tried-and-true are based on physiological and behavior change principles that have been around for some time. Trend diets are those that seem to be increasing in popularity over time, whether or not they are based on scientific principles, and fad diets are popular for a few years and then loose popularity quickly.

Some people believe that eating certain foods, limiting certain foods (other than high-calorie foods), eating certain foods in combination, or eating foods at certain times during the day hold mysterious keys to weight loss and are therefore willing to try new popular diets. The Truth is, any diet that restricts calories in some way will lead to short-term weight loss, but few provide long-term success. Below is a fun assignment to allow you to get a feel for recent dieting trends and fads among those you know and their reasons for trying them.

Directions:

1. Use the worksheet on the following page to survey 5 individuals you know about their dieting history. Record the gender and age of each participant. If they have tried the diet, have them rate how well it worked on a scale from 0=terrible to 5=very well.

2. When you have completed the worksheet, write a one-page discussion of your findings.

Activity 29 continued—Popular Diets

Popular Diets Worksheet

	1 Sex	1 Age	2 Sex	2 Age	3 Sex	3 Age	4 Sex	4 Age	5 Sex	5 Age		
	M	26	f	24								
	1 ever tried	1 how well worked (0-5)	2 ever tried	2 how well worked (0-5)	3 ever tried	3 how well worked (0-5)	4 ever tried	4 how well worked (0-5)	5 ever tried	5 how well worked (0-5)	Total ever tried	Total how well worked (0-5)
Atkins												
Zone												
South Beach												
Weight Watchers	5	3	3	3							8	3
Slim Fast												
Jenny Craig			3	4							3	4
Nurtisystem	3	5	2	4							5	4.5
Mediterranean												
Biggest Loser												
Sonoma												
Raw Food												
Special-K												
Rachael Ray												
Oprah												
Weigh Down												
Sugar Busters												
100-cal Packs												
21 lbs in 21 Days												
5-day Miracle												
Zero Fat												
Grapefruit												
Vegetarian	2	2									2	2
High Protein			1	3							1	3
Low Carb.			1	3							1	3
Food Combining												
Burst Cycling												
Fasting/Detox	10	4	2	4							12	4

Activity 30—Weight Loss Programs

Some people want more than just a diet plan; they want an entire program, perhaps with support, counseling, peers etc. Some of these plans have become quite popular in recent years. There is great variety in what they offer and what they cost. This activity will allow you to discover what some of the more popular programs offer.

Directions:

One. Select 3 programs from the following list. Try to choose programs you believe are very different.

Medifast	*NutriSystem*	*Weight Watchers*
Real Life	*Great Shapes*	*Jenny Craig*
Zumba	*Richard Simmons*	*L.A. Weightloss*
Curves	*Optifast*	*Overeaters Anonymous*
Health Management Resources (HMR)		
Take Off Pounds Sensibly (TOPS)		

Two. Use an internet search engine (e.g., *Google, Yahoo*) to locate the "official site" for each program. Additionally, use the telephone "yellow pages," or online "yellow pages," to find the nearest program to you. You will likely need to call a local program director to answer some of the questions in the worksheet.

Three. After completing the worksheet for the 3 programs, in one page, describe which plan you would most likely recommend for different individuals whom you know and why. Discuss which plan *you* would be mostly likely to use.

Worksheet—Weightloss Programs

PROGRAMS	1:	2:	3:
Do they provide food? (explain)			
Do they have regular meetings? (explain)			
Do participants interact with other participants? (explain)			

Worksheet—Weightloss Programs cont.

PROGRAMS	1:	2:	3:
Is there some form of professional counseling? (explain)			
Is there any medical supervision? (explain)			
Do they provide dieting resources? (explain)			

Worksheet—Weightloss Programs cont.

PROGRAMS	1:	2:	3:
Do they provide exercise resources? (explain)			
If you followed their plan completely for 1 month, how much would it cost? (explain)			
How many participants in local group? (explain)			
What is the approach to weight loss? (explain)			

Activity 31—Fitness Level

What does it mean to be fit? Are you fit? How do you know? Fitness can refer to heart and blood vessel condition, breathing capacity, strength, endurance, flexibility, or body composition.

- **Aerobic fitness** relates to the heart, blood vessels, and lungs working together to deliver oxygen-rich blood to the muscles during exercise. Aerobic fitness is associated with lower risk for several diseases, including hypertension and coronary heart disease.

- **Muscular strength and endurance** are both critical to your health and ability to carry out daily activities, both household tasks (yard work, carrying groceries) and job-related tasks (lifting or moving heavy objects).

- **Flexibility** implies good joint function, allowing you to walk, lift, and step normally. The ability to move a joint through its normal range of motion is affected by the muscles and connective tissues surrounding the joint. A tight muscle limits the joint's ability to move normally.

- **Body composition** refers to the ratio of lean body mass to fat, and where they are distributed in the body. The most common measure is the Body Mass Index (BMI), a number based on a person's weight and height. It can be used to identify people at risk for some diseases.

It's difficult to precisely measure each of these, but this activity will give you approximate measures of each type of fitness by completing the *President's Adult Fitness Challenge*, plus a couple additional measures.

Directions:

In the pages that follow, are instructions for each fitness test. Follow them exactly, recording your results on the worksheet at the end. It is best not to do all the tests on the same day; spread them across 2 or 3 days.

Resting Blood Pressure

Blood pressure can be affected by time of day, walking, being sick, menstruation and other factors. Ideally, you should average your readings for 3 different measures done at different times on different days. If you do not have access to a blood pressure device, find a local drug store that has a free machine. Take your reading after you have been sitting for a few minutes.

Resting Pulse

As with blood pressure, heart rate can be affected by activity, daily cycles or health. Average you readings from three different measures. Take a reading in the evening after sitting for some time; take a 2nd reading in the morning before getting out of bed; take a 3rd reading mid day after sitting for some time.

Press the index and middle fingers of your right hand firmly to the carotid artery just to the side of the Adams Apple in the neck. For 30 seconds, time the number of beats. Multiply this number by two to get your one-minute heart rate. Average the three readings.

Body Composition--BMI

Use *Step 1* from *Activity 28—Body Weight* to calculate your Body Mass Index (BMI). The BMI score is valid for both men and women, but it does have some limitations: 1) It may overestimate body fat in athletes and others, who have a muscular build, and 2) It may underestimate body fat in older persons and others who have lost muscle mass.

Am I healthy enough to take the fitness portion of the test?

The risk associated with exercise or exercise testing varies with a person's health status. Exercise testing performed on healthy adults results in a low number of abnormal cardiovascular events (e.g., dizziness, fainting, irregular heartbeats, and rarely, heart attack). The same tests performed on adults with certain diseases or risk factors place them in a higher-risk category for cardiovascular events. However, the overall risk from exercise testing in adults is low, with about 6 abnormal cardiovascular events per 10,000 people tested.

American Heart Association Physical Activity Readiness Questionnaire

If you mark any of the following statements, talk with your physician or other appropriate health care provider before engaging in exercise.

___ I have a heart condition and my health care professional recommends only medically supervised physical activity.

___ During or right after I exercise, I often have pains or pressure in my neck, left shoulder, or arm.

___ I have developed chest pain within the last month.

___ I tend to lose consciousness or fall over due to dizziness.

___ I feel extremely breathless after mild exertion.

___ My health care provider recommended that I take medicine for high blood pressure or a heart condition.

___ I have bone or joint problems that limit my ability to do moderate-intensity physical activity.

___ I have a medical condition or other physical reason not mentioned here that might need special attention in an exercise program.

___ I am pregnant and my health care professional hasn't given me the OK to be physically active.

This physical activity readiness questionnaire from the President's Challenge website is part of the American Heart Association's (AHA) Start Program. The questionnaire is available for use with the President's Challenge with permission of the AHA.

Aerobic Fitness--1-Mile Walk

Alert! *We suggest that you DO NOT take this test unless you are able to routinely walk for 15 to 20 minutes several times per week.*

To complete the one-mile walk test, you must be able to take your pulse. Your pulse can be found on the inside of your wrist just at the base of your thumb or in your neck to the side of your Adam's apple (see *Resting Pulse* test)

Equipment/Test Setting

For this test, you must walk at a brisk speed for one mile (4 laps around a standard quarter-mile track located at many schools and in some parks). We recommend that you do the test with a partner who can help with timing and recording the results. When you take the walk test, you will need to have a stop watch to start at the beginning of the test and stop at the finish line. Your partner will need to have a separate watch with a second hand so he or she can count off 10 seconds while you count your pulse rate for 10 seconds, immediately as you cross the finish line.

This test can also be performed on a treadmill. When walking on the treadmill, be sure to let your arms swing freely at your sides (do not hold on to the handrails). Keep the incline of the treadmill level (at zero). You or your partner need to record the time on the treadmill when you complete 1 mile and then follow steps 4-7 below.

Directions:

1. Walker starts the stopwatch to begin the one-mile walk.
2. The partner counts the laps and lets the walker know how many laps are left.
3. The walker stops the stopwatch while crossing the finish line.
4. The walker finds his/her pulse immediately and the partner provides a 10-second count using the stopwatch ("*Ready, begin,*" 10 seconds, "*Stop*").
5. The partner records the pulse rate for 10 seconds and multiplies by six to have heart rate in beats per minute.
6. The partner records the time for the one-mile walk in minutes and seconds.
7. The walker completes one more lap at a slower speed to "cool-down."

Muscle Strength--The Half Sit-Up Test

A common measure of muscle strength is abdominal muscle strength and endurance. You will follow the "YMCA Half Sit-Up" test, which involves lifting your trunk only partially off the floor.

Equipment/Test Setting:

You will need: 1) a Mat or rug, 2) a stopwatch or watch with a second hand, and 3) four strips of tape to place 3.5 inches apart on mat or rug to provide start and end position for the curl-up. Prepare the mat or rug with the tape strips as shown in the picture. You need to be able to feel the tape as your fingers move across the mat or rug from the starting and ending positions. We recommend that you do the test with a partner.

Directions:

1. Lie face-up on mat or rug with knees at a right angle (that is, 90º) and feet flat on the ground. The feet are not held down.
2. Place palms down on the mat with the fingers touching the first piece of tape.
3. Half sit-up so that your fingers move from the first piece of tape to the second. Then return your shoulders to the mat or rug. Your head does not have to touch the surface. Keep your lower back flat on the mat during the movements (if you arch your back, it can cause injury).
4. Your partner will count the number of half sit-ups performed in one minute. Pace yourself so you can do half sit-ups for one minute. Record your results.

The half sit-up test from the YMCA Fitness Testing and Assessment Manual, 4th edition, 2000 is included in the President's Challenges with permission.

Muscular Strength--Standard or Modified Push-Up

Alert! *If you have shoulder, elbow, or wrist pain, doing this test may aggravate your condition.*

The muscles of the upper body and shoulders are another measure of muscle strength and endurance. We are going to use standard push-ups and modified push-ups as our tests.

Directions:

 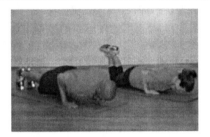

1. Males start in the standard push-up position (elevated). Hands should be shoulder width apart, arms extended straight out under the shoulders, back and legs in a straight line, and toes curled under. Females do a modified push-up with knees bent and touching the floor. Starting in the up position, hands should be slightly ahead of the shoulders so hands are in the proper position for the downward motion.
2. Lower until the chest is about 2 inches from the floor and rise up again.
3. Perform the test until you cannot complete any more push-ups while keeping your back straight and, if you are a male, keeping the legs straight as well. The key to completing the test properly is to maintain a rigid position and keep the back flat. If necessary, you can take a brief rest in the up position (not lying on the floor).
4. Record your results.

Normative data and the test protocol are included in the President's Challenge with permission of The Cooper Institute.

Flexibility—Sit-and-Reach Test

Alert! *If you have low-back pain, doing this test may aggravate it.*

One of the most common fitness tests used to measure flexibility is the Sit-and-Reach test. While not perfect, it provides some information about the hamstring and pelvis muscle groups. You will need a tape measure or yardstick, tape and a partner to help record your score.

Directions:

1. Perform a series of static stretches. These stretches should focus on stretching the trunk and legs. Following the stretches, you may also want to do some brisk walking.
2. Place a yardstick on the floor and put a long piece of masking tape over the 15 inch mark at a right angle to the yardstick.
3. Remove your shoes and sit on the floor with the yardstick between the legs (0 mark close to the "Y" of your crotch), with your feet about 12 inches apart. Heels should be at the 14 inch mark at the start of the stretch to account for the fact that the legs tend to move forward when performing the stretch.
4. With the fingertips in contact with the yardstick, slowly stretch forward with both hands as far as possible noting where the fingertips are to the closest inch. Exhaling when you stretch forward and dropping the head may allow you to stretch a bit further. Do not use fast and sudden motions, which can injure your hamstring muscles.
5. Perform the stretch three times with a few seconds of rest between stretches. Record the best measurement.

The sit and reach test is re-printed from the YMCA Fitness Testing and Assessment Manual for the President's Challenge.

Score Sheet

Gender	M
Age	20

Type of Fitness	Measure	Score		Relative Level
Cardiac	Resting Blood Pressure	108		15%
	Resting Pulse (1 min)	63		20%
Aerobic Fitness	1-Mile Walk	Time		
		HR after		
		Weight		
Muscular Strength	Half Sit-Ups (1 min)	40		35%
	Push-Ups	30		40%
Flexibility	Sit-&-Reach	12		15%
Body Composition	BMI	23		Normal

Once you have completed every test, compare your results with normative levels by entering your data online at the *President's Challenge* webpage at: *http://www.adultfitnesstest.org/dataEntry.aspx.* This will give you your percentile ranking for each measure of fitness (the 50th percentile is average). For example, the 70th percentile would mean you performed better than 70% of adults taking the test, while the 20th percentile would mean 80% performed better than you.

When you are done, in one page, discuss what you can do to improve in the areas in which you are weak.

Activity 32—Fitness Options

Some individuals are concerned that staying physically fit is difficult because of the costs associated with gym membership. Of course they could put on some shoes and go jogging, but many are unable to jog or get bored with it quickly. Is it expensive to maintain a gym membership? Would it be cheaper to set up a home gym? This activity will help you answer these questions.

Directions:

24 hour fitness

1a) Select a popular local gym (not your student recreation center) or a gym in your home town.

1b) Make a list of what equipment they have available and what classes or other services they offer with the membership (record you findings on the table that follows) *Treadmills, exercise bikes, rowers, steppers, ellipticals, free weights.*

Aerobic & Step
Cycling
Dance
Mind/Body
Strength training

1c) Determine the typical cost for full-membership for a year. *$199.99*

2a) Go to a store that carries exercise equipment (e.g., Sears, Dicks) or find online sources that show prices (e.g., *Froogle.com*, *Consumersearch.com*).

2b) Use the following table to add up how much it would cost to create a decent (but not top-of-the-line) home gym. You should include some form of aerobic exercise (e.g., stationary bike, treadmill, aerobics videos) and some form of strength training (e.g., Bowflex, free weights, push-up/pull-up bars). Consider equipment, accessories, and any instructional books or DVDs needed. Allow for some variety; but do not list equipment or materials that you would use only rarely.

3) After totaling the cost for the home gym, calculate how many years of health club membership it would take to equal your home gym cost.

4) After completing parts 1-3, in one-page, discuss which option you would prefer and why? Are there changes that could be made that would make each option more attractive? Which option do you think most people would prefer and why?

Commercial v. Home Gym Comparison Worksheet

Commercial			Home		
	Equipment	Any Added Cost		Equipment	Cost
Aerobic			Aerobic	Treadmills	$999.99
				Elliptizals	$1299.99
				Weight training	
				Dumbbells	$399.99
				Exercise bike	$449.99
Strength Training			Strength Training		
Classes or other Services			Classes or other Services		

Total Annual Cost	

Total Annual Cost	3149.96
Years of commercial gym to equal	15.8

Part Seven

Chronic Disease

Activity 33—Glycemic Index

Sometimes diabetics are simply told by their doctors that they need to avoid carbs. This is extremely difficult and may deprive them of some high-nutrient foods. In truth, it's not only the total quantity of carbohydrates in the diet that is important, but also the complexity of these carbohydrates; in other words, the speed with which carbohydrates move from the digestive tract into the blood stream.

One measure of this is called the Glycemic Index (GI). The simplest form of carbohydrate is glucose, which can move into the blood stream almost immediately. Glucose is given a score of 100 on the GI and all other carbohydrates are compared against this benchmark.

Directions:

One. In your internet browser address bar, enter: *http://glycemicindex.com/* and click on *GI Database*. (if not working use: *http://www.gilisting.com/2004/05/glycemic-index-dairy-products.html as a backup*)

Two. For each food category, identify two foods that fall within each GI level and write them in the worksheet that follows.

Three. After completing the worksheet, in one page, answer the following questions:

o Are there certain food categories diabetics must avoid? Why or Why not?

o What advice would you give a family member who is a diabetic?

	LOW (<56)	MODERATE (56-69)	HIGH (<70)
BREADS	Sourdough wheat (54) (Australia)	(65) Wholemeal barley flour bread w/ sodium propionate	Hamburger bun (Lowbaw's, (61) Toronto, Canada)
SNACKS	Chocolate, milk, plain w/ sucrose (Belgium) (34±5)	Popcorn, plain, cooked in (55±7) microwave oven	Snickers Bar (M&M/Mass, USA) (68)
CEREALS	All-Bran (39) Fruits 'n' Oats (Kellogg's, Australia)	Grapenuts (67) (Post, Kraft General Foods Inc., Toronto, Canada)	Wholemeal barley flour porridge (68) (100% regular barley
VEGETABLES	Carrots, peeled, boiled (49±2) (Sydney, NSW, Australia)	Sweet corn, boiled (60) (USA)	Type NS (67) Canada
PASTA	Capellini (45)	Macaroni & cheese, boxed (64)	Udon noodles, plain, reheated 5 min (62±8)
FRUIT	Banana (46) (Canada)	Apricots, canned in light syrup (64)	Breadfruit, raw (68)
GRAINS	Barley (22) (Canada)	Couscous, (61) boiled 5 min (Near E. Food Products Co., Leominster, Ma, USA)	Cornmeal + margarine (69)
MILK/YOGURT	Yoghurt, Type NS (Canada) (36±4)	Ice cream, NS (USA) (62)	Milk, condensed, sweetened (61±6)
BEANS	Baked beans, canned (Canada) (40±3)	Mung bean fried (Australia) (53±8)	Haricot/Navy beans, pressured cooked at 15 psi for 25 min (59)
SUGAR COMPARABLE	Fructose (in many fruits) (43)	Sucrose (table sugar) (65)	Glucose (100)

Activity 34—Arthritis Treatment

Arthritis is a painful and often debilitating condition that affects joint alignment and movement. There are more than 100 types of arthritis that can affect humans. Osteoarthritis, the most common, is typically caused by injury, overuse, or simply old age. Treatment varies depending on the type of arthritis. Common treatments include pain medication, dietary changes, exercise, physical therapy, bracing or surgery. Although newer treatments offer some relief, currently there are no cures.

Medical conditions for which there are no cures often result in questionable treatments arising outside the medical community. Some of these come from historic folk medicine; others are proposed by complementary and alternative medicine practitioners. This assignment will allow you to investigate some of these approaches to treating arthritis.

Directions:

This assignment will require you to use the Internet to search out websites regarding several interesting treatments for arthritis. Select six therapies from the following table. For each treatment, you will look for a website that promotes (encourages) the treatment and another that critiques, questions or criticizes the practice. In the worksheet that follows, for each treatment, you will write your answers to these questions:

PRO– What do proponents say about it? Why do they think it will help?

CON–What do opponents say about its validity?

RECOMMEND?–Would you recommend it? Why or why not?

Worksheet—Alternative Arthritis Treatments

	PRO	**CON**
Acupuncture		

RECOMMEND?

	PRO	CON
Apitherapy		

RECOMMEND?

	PRO	CON
Copper Bracelets		

RECOMMEND?

	PRO	CON
Corticosteroids		

RECOMMEND?

	PRO	CON
Dimethyl Sulfoxide		

RECOMMEND?

	PRO	CON
Fish Oils		

RECOMMEND?

	PRO	CON
Glucosamine & Condroitin		

RECOMMEND?

	PRO	CON
Liniments / Rubs (e.g. Bengay)		

RECOMMEND?

	PRO	CON
Magnet Therapy		

RECOMMEND?

	PRO	CON
Massage Therapy		

RECOMMEND?

	PRO	CON
Relaxation Techniques		

RECOMMEND?

	PRO	CON
Stretching and Special Exercises		

RECOMMEND?

	PRO	CON
Unique Diet or Special Foods		

RECOMMEND?

	PRO	CON
Vibrators		

RECOMMEND?

	PRO	CON
Whirlpool Baths		

RECOMMEND?

Activity 35—Genetics

Environmental, behavioral and genetic factors play a role in disease risk. This activity will help you better understand the role genetics plays in disease risk. You will also learn about the types of genetic tests available and the purposes for which they are used.

Directions

1. Read the following short explanation about genetic disorders:

The programming for the way cells and tissues grow and work is stored in the DNA. DNA is grouped in discrete bundles called chromosomes in the nucleolus of cells. We typically get half of each chromosome from each parent. Segments of chromosomes that are responsible for specific physiological functions are called genes.

Genetic disorders are sometimes due to missing or extra chromosomes, but are more often caused by abnormalities at the gene level. The most common chronic disorders, such as heart disease, Alzheimer's disease, arthritis, diabetes, cancer, and types of mental illness are multi-factorial, meaning they are caused by the interaction of multiple genes as well as personal behaviors and environment. However, mutation of a single gene can also result in disease. There are more than 6,000 known single-gene disorders, occurring in about 1 out of every 200 births. Some examples are cystic fibrosis, sickle cell anemia, and Huntington's disease.

Some genetic disorders are dominant, meaning disease will result if only half the gene pair has the trait. Others are recessive, requiring both parts of the gene pair to have the disease trait. However, these recessive traits could be passed on to children if both parents carry the recessive trait. (More information on the different modes of inheritance can be obtained at: *http://www.nlm.nih.gov/medlineplus/ency/article/002048.htm* or *http://www.gig.org.uk/education2.htm*)

2. Research any two of the following genetic disorders; be sure to select any that run in your family or for which you would be at greater risk. The following websites have excellent resources: *http://www.genome.gov/10001204*, or *http://www.wrongdiagnosis.com/g/genetic/basics.htm.*

Common Genetic Disorders

- *Color blindness (1/12 males, 1/100 females)*
- *Von Willebrand disease (1/100, mostly undiagnosed)*
- *Breast cancer (1/200 women have BCRA predisposition)*
- *Heritable Disorders of Connective Tissue (1/300)*
- *Hemochromatosis (1/500)*
- *Polycystic kidney disease (1/500)*
- *Down's Syndrome (1/600, increases with advanced maternal age)*
- *Duchenne muscular dystrophy (1/600 males)*
- *Fragile X syndrome (1/1000 males, 1/8000 females)*
- *Charcot-Marie-Tooth Disorder (1/2000)*
- *Sickle cell disease (1/3000; 1/500 African American, 1/1000 Hispanic)*
- *Cystic Fibrosis (1/3000 Caucasian Americans)*
- *Neurofibromatosis-1 (1/4000)*
- *Marfan syndrome (1/5000)*
- *Phenylketonuria (1/10,000)*
- *Hemophilia - Factor VIII Deficiency (1/20,000 males)*

---

3. Then, complete the tables that follow.

Disorder 1:	Fragile X Syndrome
Describe the disease and its symptoms	-Most common form of inherited mental retardation in males & also a significant cause in females. - 1/4000 males; 1/8000 females - Particular facial appearance: a large sized head, long face, prominent forehead & chin & protruding ears. Behavioral problems: hyperactivity, hand flapping, hand biting, temper tantrums & autism. After puberty: poor eye contact, Perseverative speech, problems in impulse control & distractibility. Physical problems: eye, orthopedic, heart, & skin problems.
How is it diagnosed?	- A genetic test (polymerase chain reaction [PCR]) can be performed to diagnose fragile X. This test looks for an expanded mutation (called a triplet repeat) in the FMR1 gene.
How can it be treated?	-No special treatment - Supportive therapy for children — special check document — MacBook

Disorder 2:	Hemophilia
Describe the disease and its symptoms	-Bleeding Disorder that slows down the blood clotting process -Hemophilia A - 1/5000 - 10,000 males worldwide -Hemophilia B - 1/20,000 - 34500 males worldwide -Prolonged oozing after injuries, tooth extractions or surgery, renewed bleeding after initial bleeding has stopped; easy bruising & prolonged bleeding.
How is it diagnosed?	- Measuring factor clotting activity - Genetic testing
How can it be treated?	Treatment may involve slow injection of a medicine called desmopressin (DDAVP) by the doctor into one of the veins.

4. Read the following short explanation of genetic testing:

Genetic tests use various laboratory techniques to determine whether a person has, or is likely to get, a genetic condition or disease. The results depend both on reliable laboratory procedures and accurate interpretation of results. When interpreting the results, one must take into account the probability of **false positive** or **false negative** test results. Special training is required to analyze and convey information about genetic testing to affected individuals. Genetic testing can be used for 5 reasons:

Carrier Identification includes genetic tests used by couples whose families have a history of recessive genetic disorders and who are considering having children. Examples of common tests for this purpose include those for cystic fibrosis, Tay-Sachs disease, and sickle-cell trait.

Prenatal Diagnosis is genetic testing of a fetus. This may occur when there is a risk of bearing a child with genes associated with mental retardation or physical deterioration. Down Syndrome is one of the most common genetic diseases screened by this method.

Newborn Screening is frequently done as a preventative health measure. Tests usually have clear benefit to the newborn because treatment is available. Phenylketonuria (PKU) and congenital hypothyroidism are conditions for which testing is conducted in most states.

Late-onset Disorders refer to diseases that aren't apparent until adulthood. These are complex conditions that have genetics, behavioral and environmental causes. Genetic tests may indicate a susceptibility or predisposition for these diseases. There are diseases caused by single genes, such as Huntington's disease, that can be tested at any time. And there are diseases, such a breast cancer, that although they have other risk factors, are strongly influences by the presence of certain genes.

Because every individual (except identical twins) has unique "DNA fingerprints," genetic testing can also be used for **identification purposes.** It can be used in legal cases involving paternity, criminal investigations, and to identify those who have died in accidents, disasters, or war.

5. Go to the following website and read the personal story about genetic testing. *http://www.ourbodiesourselves.org/book/companion.asp?id=28&compID=28* After reading the story, answer the questions that follow.

Questions

A) What factors affected her decision?

B) What would you have done under the same circumstances? (if you are male, pretend its testicular cancer at issue)

C) You are expecting your 3rd child later in life. Because of your age (or your wife's age) the obstetrician is recommending that you have a test for Down's syndrome. What would you do?

Activity 35 continued—Genetics

Activity 36—Leading Causes of Death

A century ago in the United States (and currently in many developing countries) the leading causes of death were from infectious diseases, such as respiratory, diarrheal, malarial and tubercular infections. Today in most developed countries the leading causes of death are from chronic diseases that usually develop over years and are partly caused by lifestyle. The top 10 causes of death in 2006, according to the U.S. Centers for Disease Control and Prevention, are listed below. (For more details go to: *http://www.cdc.gov/nchs/FASTATS/lcod.htm)*. Six of the ten can be considered chronic diseases (1-4, 6, and 9). This activity will help you better understand factors that increase risk for these diseases and steps that could be taken in adulthood to reduce these risks.

1. Heart disease: 631,636
2. Cancer: 559,888
3. Stroke (cerebrovascular diseases): 137,119
4. Chronic lower respiratory diseases: 124,583
5. Accidents (unintentional injuries): 121,599
6. Diabetes: 72,449
7. Alzheimer's disease: 72,432
8. Influenza and Pneumonia infections: 56,326
9. Kidney Disease (nephritic conditions): 45,344
10. Septicemia infections: 34,234

Directions

a) Go online and read the following short articles regarding risk factors for five leading chronic diseases.

Heart Disease: *http://www.cdc.gov/HeartDisease/risk_factors.htm*

Cancer: *http://www.cancer.gov/cancertopics/wyntk/overview/page4*

Stroke: *http://www.cdc.gov/stroke/risk_factors.htm*

Diabetes: *http://www.nlm.nih.gov/medlineplus/ency/article/002072.htm*

Kidney Disease: *http://www.mayoclinic.com/health/kidney-failure/DS00682/DSECTION=risk-factors*

---

b) Imagine that you were planning a presentation to a group of college students on how to lower their risk for these five chronic diseases. Using information you have gleaned from the web articles, complete the table below, which you will use in your presentation. List all the common risk factors and note which diseases they affect.

c) Identify factors they don't need to worry about because they can't be changed, factors that can be controlled by individual behavior changes, and factors that society or the government could address to lower everyone's risk.

d) Place an asterisk (*) to the left of the most important risk factors.

e) Estimate how expensive it will be for individuals or society, where necessary, to change the risk factor ($=no or low expense, $$=moderately expensive, $$$=very expensive).

Importance	Risk Factor	Heart Disease	Cancer	Stroke	Diabetes	Kidney Disease	Can't Control	Individual Control	What could society do to lower risk?	Cost to change
l	Blood cholesterol levels	√						√	Eat foods w/ less cholesterol	$$
	Tobacco Use	√						√	Stop smoking / foods w/ less fat a "	$$
l	Tobacco		√					√	Quit smoking	$
	Alcohol		√					√	Don't drink a lot.	$
l	High blood pressure			√				l	smoking, diets high in salt, alcohol	$$$
	Physical inactivity			√				√	Exercise more	$
	low activity level				√			√	exercise	$
	excess body weight				√			√	exercise	$
l	Family history					√	√			$$$
	Race					√	√			$$$

Activity 37—Family Tree of Health

Chronic diseases are unique in that they are partly due to lifestyle, but also partly related to genetics. This does not mean that if your parents or family members have the disease you are doomed to have it; it simply means you are at greater risk for the condition. Without testing for specific genes, it's not possible to precisely know your genetic risk. However, knowing something about what members of your family have experienced will at least give you a hint of these genetic risks. Knowing you are at greater risk may provide the motivation to alter lifestyle to reduce your risk.

<u>Directions:</u>

For this activity, you will need to talk to your parents and perhaps other extended family members. Your goal is to discover health information about your parents, grandparents, uncles and aunts, whether they are living or dead. The *Family Tree of Health* does not include all possible diseases of concern, but a sample of the conditions that are associated with the leading causes of mortality (death) or morbidity (suffering). Find out whether each individual on the chart has ever been diagnosed with the listed condition.

If you are male, you are interested in male cancers, such as testicular or prostate; don't record the female cancers. If you are female, record female cancers, such as breast, cervical, ovarian, or uterine.

In the boxes for uncles and aunts, record the total number of uncles and aunts on each side and the number with each condition (again only the gender cancers that are appropriate for your gender).

Once you have completed the *Family Tree of Health*, write a one-page summary of your findings and what steps you could take to lower your risks.

Family Tree of Health

Grandpa __2__
- ___heart disease
- ___stroke
- _1_ diabetes
- _1_ prostate cancer
- ___other cancer

Grandma __1__
- ___heart disease
- ___stroke
- ✓ diabetes
- ___breast cancer
- ___other cancer

Grandpa __5__
- ___heart disease
- ___stroke
- ___diabetes
- ___prostate cancer
- _1_ other cancer

Grandma __6__
- ___heart disease
- ___stroke
- ___diabetes
- ___breast cancer
- _1_ other cancer

_4_ # uncles/aunts
- ___# heart disease
- ___# stroke
- _1_# diabetes
- ___# prostate cancer
- ___# breast cancer
- _1_# other cancer

Dad
- ___heart disease
- ___stroke
- _1_ diabetes
- ___prostate cancer
- ___other cancer

Mom
- ___heart disease
- ___stroke
- ___diabetes
- ___breast cancer
- _1_ other cancer

_3_ # uncles/aunts
- ___# heart disease
- ___# stroke
- ___# diabetes
- ___# prostate cancer
- ___# breast cancer
- ___# other cancer

Your Risk
- ____heart disease
- ____stroke
- _1_ diabetes
- ____gender cancer
- _1_ other cancer

Count the # of times each condition appeared and divide by the total number of relatives (parents count double for conditions). Then label your risk for each.

V high = more than half	
High = more than 1/3	
Moderate = more than 1/4	
Low = less than 1/4	

Consumer Health Activities

Activity 38—Cancer Screening

Cancer is a category of diseases characterized by changes, leading to uncontrolled cell growth in various tissues. Cancer, like other chronic diseases, is affected by genetics, lifestyle, and various exposures. There are similarities among the types of cancers, but there are also differences in terms of risk factors. For example, some cancers are strongly related to exposure, while others are strongly associated with family history. The most common cancers in the United States are listed in the table below. This activity will allow you to assess your risk for the most common types of cancer.

Directions

A very thorough and user-friendly screening tool is available online from the Washington University School of Medicine. Access this site by typing the following address into your web browser: _http://www.yourdiseaserisk .wustl.edu/hccpquiz.pl?lang=english&func=home&page=cancer index_ (If for some reason this is not working, try a similar tool from the Harvard School of Public Health at: _http://www.diseaseriskindex.harvard.edu/update/ hccpquiz.pl?lang=english&func=home&page=cancer index_)

Use the online screening tool to assess your current level of risk for the following types of cancer for your gender:

Women	lung, colon, pancreatic, melanoma, breast
Men	lung, colon, pancreatic, melanoma, prostate

After completing the screenings, answer questions that follow:

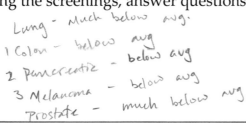

Lung - Much below avg.
1 Colon - below avg
2 Pancreatic - below avg
3 Melanoma - below avg
Prostate - much below avg

QUESTIONS

➜ For which types of cancers did you have the greatest risk? Why do you believe this is the case?

The type of cancer that I had ẓ the greatest risk is colon cancer. I believe this is the case because I don't take aspirin, calcium supplements, or dairy foods, and multivitamins every week

➜ Were there any suggestions for lowering your risk for any of the types of cancer?

The suggestions given for lowering risk for any of the types of cancer was more exercise, taking vitamins, and eat fruits & vegetables.

➜ What were the common suggestions across all type of cancer for keeping your risk low?

Common suggestions across all type of cancer for keeping my risk low were exercising and eating fruits & vegetables.

➜ What changes will you consider making at this point in your life to reduce your risks of cancer?

I would exercise more, eat more servings of fruits & vegetables, and take vitamins.

Activity 39—Cancer Risks

Many people, particularly young people, are not aware of the risks associated with developing cancer. Suppose you were asked to develop a short questionnaire that could help them identify their level of risk and perhaps motivate them to visit their physicians for further screening. Perhaps this questionnaire could be given out in classrooms, doctors' offices, malls or other public places.

Directions:

Your questionnaire should meet the following guidelines:

- ✓ Assesses major risk factors for the most common type of cancers (lung, breast, colon, etc.)

- ✓ Could be given to adults of various ages, genders, and cultures

- ✓ Could be completed in a short time (10 or fewer questions)

- ✓ Questions are weighted according to the magnitude of each risk factor

- ✓ Questionnaire provides a total score that could identify, at minimum: high, moderate and low risk.

You will need to get online (e.g., _webmd.com_, _mayoclinic.com_) to look up the primary risk factors that are common for the most significant cancers. Some will be unique to certain cancers, some will overlap.

Use the table on the next page to outline your questionnaire.

Cancer Questionnaire

| Question | LEVEL | | |
	0 pts	1 pts	2 pts
1 How often do you drink alcohol ?	0	1-4	5+
2 For how long do you exercise ?	30 min	1 hr	3 hrs
3 How many times do you smoke tobacco a day?	0	1-4	5+
4 How often do you have diets high in salt?	0	1-9	10+
5 How many family members had cancer?	0	<10	>10
6 How long do you stand in sunlight ?	few minutes	Sometimes	All the time
7 Have you been exposed to chemicals?	No	"	Many times
8 How often do you wash your hands	Always	"	Rarely
9			
10			
TOTAL SCORE	24		

KEY	
LOW RISK:	<
MODERATE RISK:	
HIGH RISK:	>

Activity 40—Living with Cancer

There was a time when a diagnosis of cancer was an unavoidable death sentence. Today, with early identification and modern treatments, many types of cancer are survivable. However, the experience is still difficult and often involves suffering. For this activity, you will contact a family member (or someone else) who has been diagnosed with cancer. Respectfully, ask them to answer the following questions regarding their experience.

1) Other than genetics, do you believe you could have done anything to avoid getting cancer? Please explain:

2) What type of treatments have you received? Do you think they have worked or are working? Why do you believe this?

3) How has the cancer treatment, and/or changes in your own behaviors, affected your lifestyle and quality of life?

4) Has your mental/emotional state or your life philosophy changed since being diagnosed?

5) What advice would you give to young adults?

Part Eight

Drugs and Alcohol

Activity 41—Over-the-Counter Drugs

What's the difference between "name brand" and "store brand"non-prescription medications? Find out.

Directions:

Go to a store that carries "store brands" (e.g., CVS (CVS brand), Walgreens (Wal-green brand), Walmart (Equate brand), almost every store nowadays). Choose two different categories of drugs (cough medicine, pain relievers, decongestants, sleep aids, allergy medicine, etc.). For each category, identify the "name brand" and the equivalent "store brand" version of a product. Use the table on the next page to record the following information:

❖ The product, its size, and its cost for both the name and store brands

❖ Calculate the cost per same size dose for each product.

❖ For both products, list the active ingredients in order and then inactive ingredients in order.

❖ Briefly describe what each ingredient does. Refer to a medical textbook (Physician Desk Reference) or one of these web sites (*rxlist.com, healthtouch.com , medscape.com*) to find this information.

After completing the table, answer the following questions:

A. What did you learn from this activity?

B. Why do you think "name brands" sell better than "store brands?"

Product 1 Comparison

Name Brand:	Neutrogena Sensitive skin ~~block~~ sun block		
Product & size		Retail price	Cost per dose
bottle 4 3 oz		$9.49	$3.99
List of Ingredients		Function of Ingredients	
water		moisture	
Titanium dioxide		pigment (color)	
Camellia Oleifera		Green tea smell	
Calcium pantothenate		Vitamin B5 (nutrition)	

Store Brand:	CVS Sunscreen Lotion, Family size		
Product & size		Retail price	Cost per dose
sunscreen bottle, 16 oz		$9.99	$3.49
List of Ingredients		Function of Ingredients	
fragrance		allergies / immunotoxicity	
Aloe vera gel		nutrition	
water		moisture	

Product 2 Comparison

Name Brand:			
Product & size		Retail price	Cost per dose
List of Ingredients	Function of Ingredients		

Store Brand:			
Product & size		Retail price	Cost per dose
List of Ingredients	Function of Ingredients		

Activity 41 continued—Over-the-Counter Drugs

Activity 42—Drug Messages on TV

Television advertising for medication, both prescription and over-the-counter, has become a huge business. Companies not only need to cover the costs of research, production and distribution, but also these advertising expenses. Most Over-the-Counter drugs (OTC) and many prescription medications have competitors trying to capture the same market. These conditions have led drug companies to hire advertising agencies and to get more aggressive with their marketing. This activity will give you a feel for the categories of drugs that are most heavily marketed and the promotional approaches they use.

Directions:

For this assignment, you will watch two hours of broadcast television and analyze the amounts and types of advertising for medicine. Limit yourself to the following channels: ABC, CBS, FOX, and NBC.

I. Select a time of day and day of the week. For general adults, you will watch between 8 pm and 11 pm on a weekday evening. Alternatively, you could choose to focus on a two-hour period during the day, between 10 am and 3 pm.

II. While you watch, use the worksheet on the following page to record information about drug advertisements. Pay attention not only to the words, but also to the implied meanings.

III. After completing the worksheet for two hours of programming, answer the questions on page 180.

TV Drug Messages Worksheet

Time	Channel	Program	Company	Drug	OTC
10·AM	ABC -7			Tylenol	Prescription
Summary of message:					
Headaches and pain will go away, giving relief					
Time	Channel	Program	Company	Drug	OTC
10:30 ~~10:45~~ AM	CBS - 2			Aleve	prescription
Summary of message:					
2 pills a day gives relief for 24 hours					
Time	Channel	Program	Company	Drug	OTC
11:45 ~~11:30~~	FOX 11			Advil	prescription
Summary of message:					
Advil Liquidgel will provide relief every 4 hours					
Time	Channel	Program	Company	Drug	OTC
					prescription
Summary of message:					
Time	Channel	Program	Company	Drug	OTC
					prescription
Summary of message:					
Time	Channel	Program	Company	Drug	OTC
					prescription
Summary of message:					

TV Drug Messages Worksheet

Time	Channel	Program	Company	Drug	OTC prescription
Summary of message:					
Time	Channel	Program	Company	Drug	OTC prescription
Summary of message:					
Time	Channel	Program	Company	Drug	OTC prescription
Summary of message:					
Time	Channel	Program	Company	Drug	OTC prescription
Summary of message:					
Time	Channel	Program	Company	Drug	OTC prescription
Summary of message:					
Time	Channel	Program	Company	Drug	OTC prescription
Summary of message:					

TV Drug Messages Worksheet

Time	Channel	Program	Company	Drug	OTC prescription
Summary of message:					
Time	Channel	Program	Company	Drug	OTC prescription
Summary of message:					
Time	Channel	Program	Company	Drug	OTC prescription
Summary of message:					
Time	Channel	Program	Company	Drug	OTC prescription
Summary of message:					
Time	Channel	Program	Company	Drug	OTC prescription
Summary of message:					
Time	Channel	Program	Company	Drug	OTC prescription
Summary of message:					

Consumer Health Activities

TV Drug Messages Worksheet

Time	Channel	Program	Company	Drug	OTC prescription
Summary of message:					
Time	Channel	Program	Company	Drug	OTC prescription
Summary of message:					
Time	Channel	Program	Company	Drug	OTC prescription
Summary of message:					
Time	Channel	Program	Company	Drug	OTC prescription
Summary of message:					
Time	Channel	Program	Company	Drug	OTC prescription
Summary of message:					
Time	Channel	Program	Company	Drug	OTC prescription
Summary of message:					

Questions

Did anything surprise you?

That Aleve is better than Tylenol and Advil combined

How many commercials were about drugs?

3 that were different, 10 total

What prescription drug categories were most advertised? What over-the-counter drug categories were most advertised?

Aleve

What were the dominate messages? What were the implied messages?

Taking 2 Aleve pills a day gives relief for 24 hours. 2 pills would equal to 4 pills of the leading otc drug brands

Should there be changes in what is allowed to be presented on television about drugs? If yes, what?

No, there does not need to be changes because all commercials are appropriate

Activity 43—Alcohol Messages

Alcohol is the most common drug of choice in the United States and many other countries. Though it has psychomotor effects on the body and brain, culturally it's often treated differently than other drugs. We allow advertising and promotion for types of alcohol in television, radio, print media, and other outlets. This activity will make you aware of the type of messages that are communicated about alcohol.

Directions:

For this activity, you will watch two hours of broadcast television analyzing the amount and type of messages related to alcohol. Limit yourself to the following channels: ABC, CBS, FOX, or NBC.

I. Select a day of the week and a time of day. For general adults, you will watch between 8 pm and 11 pm on a weekday evening. Alternatively, you could choose to focus on a two-hour period during the day between 10 am and 3 pm.

II. While you watch, use the worksheets on the following pages to record alcohol messages. Enjoy the programs, but don't get so involved that you miss subtle alcohol messages. Look for messages in commercials as well as the entertainments shows. Pay attention not only to the words, but also to the implied messages. For each advertisement, note which primary persuasion themes are used (sometimes more than one) and to which segments of society the ad would most appeal.

III. After completing the worksheet, answer the questions on page 186.

Worksheets—Alcohol Messages on TV

| Day of week: | Monday | Time: | 10:00 AM – 12: PM |

Character (or sponsor if a commercial)	themes or techniques used							to whom would it appeal		
	sex appeal	humor	success	seems fun	social bonds	relaxing	beverage taste	adults	college	minor
Police department			√				√	√	√	√
DUI							√	√	√	√
Health and Safety		√				√		√	√	√

Worksheets—Alcohol Messages on TV

Day of week:	Time:

Character (or sponsor if a commercial)	themes or techniques used							to whom would it appeal		
	sex appeal	humor	success	seems fun	social bonds	relaxing	beverage taste	adults	college	minor

Worksheets—Alcohol Messages on TV

Day of week:	Time:

Character (or sponsor if a commercial)	themes or techniques used							to whom would it appeal		
	sex appeal	humor	success	seems fun	social bonds	relaxing	beverage taste	adults	college	minor

Worksheets—Alcohol Messages on TV

Day of week:	Time:

Character (or sponsor if a commercial)	themes or techniques used							to whom would it appeal		
	sex appeal	humor	success	seems fun	social bonds	relaxing	beverage taste	adults	college	minor

Questions

1) Did anything surprise you?

No, because I know that drinking is bad
and too much is unhealthy.

2) How many alcohol messages were given?

1 about drinking, 5 about drinking & driving

3) What were the dominate themes or persuasion techniques?
What were the implied messages?

Telling us that drinking and driving is dangerous.
If you drink too much, ask someone to drive you
or take a cab.

4) What could be misleading about some of these themes? Which
themes would appeal to adults, college students, and minors?

Some of these commercials are trying to show
people that some alcoholic drinks are better than
others when they aren't or if its they're are same and it can bring out
a different outcome

5) Should there be changes in what is allowed to be presented
regarding alcohol? If yes, what?

Yes there should be changes because
some of the commercials are showing
some people drinking too much and the law
taking the wrong people that are not at fault.

Part Nine

Health and Beauty Products

Activity 44—Health and Beauty Aids

What scares people most? One common answer would be growing old. We will try almost anything to be younger looking or more attractive. Many of the products advertised on television, in magazines, or sold in drug stores and mass merchandise stores can be grouped in the category called Health and Beauty Aids (HBA). Most of these products are for either skin (moisture, texture, perspiration, acne, appearance, etc.) or hair (scalp, texture, appearance, shine, strength, dandruff, etc.). With this activity, you will research one such product and what others believe about it.

Directions:

One.   Select a HBA product that has one or more explicit or implied claims to enhance appearance or youthful look in some way (perhaps something you have in your home and/or something in which you once believed).

Two.   Research the primary ingredients in the product using Internet databases such as *cosmeticsdatabase.com*. Record the primary uses, effects, and any potential negative side effects of the primary ingredients.

Three. Ask around to find two individuals who have used the same product (or a similar product with the same ingredients). Ask them to what degree they believe the product's claims; what motivated them to purchase the product; and why they use or have used it?

Four.   Tell these individuals what you learned about the ingredients and about the product's claims. If there is any negative information, ask them whether they will continue to use the product after hearing this information. If yes, why?

Five.   In one page, discuss your findings.

Ingredients and Effects

Name: Pantene Pro-V Fine Hair Solutions : Fragile to Strong		
Product & size	Retail price	Cost per dose
replenishes and nourishes hair from root (12.6 oz)	$29.94	$2.94

List of Ingredients	Effects of Ingredients
Water	
Cetyl Alcohol	
Citric Acid	
Methylchloroisothaizolinone	
Fragrance	Smell
Panthenol	

Questions about HBA Product Use

Why they bought the product? Why they use it?

Respondent 1	Respondent 2
The bought this product because they wanted to use a product that would make her hair feel fuller and no tangles. She used this product because its gentle, improve hair health & texture, smells great, and smooths and softens.	

Questions about HBA Product Use continued

How much they believe the claims?

Respondent 1	Respondent 2
She believes the claims because Pantene is a popular product and the always work, so trying a new product from them won't disappoint.	

What they think of your information? Will they continue using it why or why not?

Respondent 1	Respondent 2
She thinks that my information is pretty much the basic idea on how the product works. She will continue to use the product and will recommend others to use it because it worked for her and she was happy with this product	

Activity 44 continued—Health and Beauty Aides

Activity 45—HBA Experiment

This assignment will involve experimenting with a Health or Beauty Aide (HBA) product to test its claims. Think of it as a scientific experiment with only one subject—you.

Directions:

Choose an HBA product for which you have been curious, but never tried. Most of these products are designed to improve the condition or appearance of your skin or hair. Make sure you choose something for which there is potential of noticing some results within 7 days (seek approval from your instructor before beginning). DO NOT choose something that will interfere with any current treatment or put you at risk in any way.

Once you have selected the technique, you will take the following steps:

1st.　　Develop the methods for your experiment: How will you control for other variables? How will you be able to measure if it worked? To what will you compare your results?

2nd.　　Use the product as recommended for at least 7 days.

3rd.　　Keep a daily diary of your skin or hair condition, as well as any potential side effects.

4th.　　Answer the questions on the following page.

Questions about HBA Experiment

❖ Describe your experiment methods.

❖ Describe your results.

❖ In your opinion, are the claims valid? Why or why not?

❖ If you were to design a *real* scientific experiment to study this product, what would it look like?

Activity 46—Infomercials

Infomercials are a unique category of programming. They are designed to look like informational programs, scripted and cast to be entertaining, yet most are paid advertising for the purpose of selling a product or service. Some offer products or services that are similar to what is available through other distributions channels, others claim to be unique in some way. Many are of questionable benefit. With this activity, you will analyze the claims of a typical infomercial.

Directions:

a) Watch and/or record a health-related television infomercial. Most of these will appear on broadcast channels (ABC, CBS, FOX, and NBC) during non-primetime hours (usually middle of the day or after midnight). They are often about topics such as: weight loss, hair replacement, skin conditioning, muscle building, super nutrition, and other topics.

b) Carefully record: 1) the claims made by the promoters, 2) the evidence given to support the claims, and 3) the credentials for those who developed the product or service.

c) Use the Internet and the library (or online library journal databases) to find studies regarding these claims (include at least one academic source and one Internet source).

d) Most claims are founded on at least a grain of truth. Find this grain of truth. What is true about their claims?

e) Find at least one credible study that refutes or clarifies these claims.

f) Answer the questions on the following page.

Questions about Infomercial

1) Briefly describe the infomercial, the product, and its claims.

The infomercial talked about the Proactiv acne solution and washing your face with it will have the combination of medicines to attack the bacteria source.

2) What about the claims is correct?

The acne solution directly attacks the bacteria source, and which is small buildup of dirt that clogs the pores, and prevents future break outs.

3) Based on your research, what about the claims is incorrect or exaggerated?

I did not find a claim that was either incorrect or exaggerated for this product.

4) What do you think is the motivation for this promotion?

The motivation for this promotion is that there are many people w/ acne problems and being a well-known brand, it should sell quickly.

5) Who is likely to buy it?

People who have use proactiv before or people that tried many products other than proactiv that were not satisfied.

6) What changes could be made in the product or promotion that would make it more credible and more beneficial?

Changes that could be made is showing the steps of how to use the product and how long it will take to see results.

Part Ten

Sexual and Reproductive Health

Activity 47—Pregnancy and Child Birth

One of the most fundamental and dramatic experiences in life can be carrying or bringing a child into the world. What happens during pregnancy and delivery can have important health consequences for both the child and the mother. Although the experience is natural, occurring since the beginning of man, the process is now considered a medical condition that is carefully monitored and treated to create the best possible outcome for the mother and child. This activity will give you some understanding of the modern experience of pregnancy and childbirth.

Directions:

Although expectant mothers have several choices; including unsupervised pregnancy and delivery, water birthing, hypno-birth, etc.; this activity will focus on the 2 most common approaches in this country: obstetrician supervised births and midwifery.

First—complete the following table regarding typical costs. You will need to call a local midwife and a local obstetrician's office. Assume no insurance. For the obstetrician's office, ask how costs and procedures would differ for a high-risk pregnancy (e.g., one requiring a Cesarean delivery)

	Typical Low-Risk Pregnancy		High-Risk Pregnancy
	Midwife	Obstetrician	Obstetrician
Cost of initial visit	$ 2,000	$2,000	$4000
Typical # of visits during the pregnancy	30	30	50
Cost of visits during pregnancy	$ 200	$ 200	$ 350
Typical # and kind of tests run during pregnancy (e.g., urine, blood, imaging)	10	10	15
Cost of all tests run during pregnancy	$ 2,000	$ 2,000	$ 4,500
Cost of delivery for physician or midwife	$ 5000	$5000	$ 7,500
Cost of delivery Cesarean birth	███		$ 33,000
Cost of delivery for hospital (if applicable)	$ 8,000	$8000	$10,000
Cost of delivery for anesthesiologist (if applicable)	$ 15,000	$ 15,000	$ 15,000
Cost of hospital stay (if applicable)	$50,000	$ 50,000	$ 50,000
Total Cost	$ 82,000	$82,000	$ 125,350

Second—Interview three women regarding their experiences during pregnancy, during child birth, and immediately after birth. Select one who used a midwife, one who used an obstetrician, and one who had a high risk pregnancy with a cesarean delivery. Ask each the questions on the following page.

MOTHER INTERVIEW ONE (MIDWIFE CARE)

1. What did you like about the care you received during your pregnancy?

   The care that she received during pregnancy was good because she was well taken care of and got the help she needed.

2. What did you not like or what would you have done differently?

   She didn't like the environment too much, but most of the people there were nice enough to help her.

3. How was your relationship with your midwife?

   Her relationship w/ the midwife was okay because sometimes she would talk too fast and I couldn't understand.

4. Did you or your baby have any problems during your pregnancy or delivery? If yes, how were these problems treated?

   No, there ~~weren't too~~ were no problems during the delivery.

5. What advice would you give to a newly expectant mother?

   She would tell be to be calm and take deep breaths. If she would do something that she is not supposed to do, the baby would get hurt.

6. What advice would you give to the expectant father (or other pregnancy/delivery companion)?

   She would tell the companion that he needs to be there for her at all times.

MOTHER INTERVIEW TWO (OBSTETRICIAN CARE)

1. What did you like about the care you received during your pregnancy?

2. What did you not like or what would you have done differently?

3. How was your relationship with your physician?

4. Did you or your baby have any problems during your pregnancy or delivery? If yes, how were these problems treated?

5. What advice would you give to a newly expectant mother?

6. What advice would you give to the expectant father (or other pregnancy/delivery companion)?

MOTHER INTERVIEW THREE (HIGH-RISK)

1. What did you like about the care you received during your pregnancy?

2. What did you not like or what would you have done differently?

3. How was your relationship with your physician?

4. Did you or your baby have any problems during your pregnancy or delivery? If yes, how were these problems treated?

5. What advice would you give to a newly expectant mother?

6. What advice would you give to the expectant father (or other pregnancy/delivery companion)?

Activity 47 continued—Pregnancy and Child Birth

Activity 48—Contraception

Contraception is the prevention of pregnancy during intercourse. With modern technology, there are a variety of methods from which to choose. These methods have varied failure rates and unique advantages and disadvantages. They also vary widely in what they cost. This assignment will help you understand the various methods that are available and the pro and cons of each method.

Directions:

Complete the table on the following pages. Most of the information is available online. (Examples: *http://www.contracept.org/risks.phphttp://* OR *www.contraceptivetechnology.com/table.html*).

You will need to look up:

- A description of each method
- The failure rate with typical/average use
- Whether the method also protects from contracting STDs
- Whether the method can be acquired over the counter (OTC) or requires a prescription

From what you have read, determine the following:

- Who is primarily responsible for the contraception: the man, the women, or either?
- How convenient the contraceptive would be to use regularly? (give a rating of *good, moderate,* or *poor* convenience)
- Whether the method would cause some discomfort? (give a rating of *good, moderate,* or *poor* comfort)
- List any additional advantages (pros) and disadvantages (cons), including side-effects for each method.

Finally, determine the typical cost for using each procedure, most of this can be learned from a pharmacist, but you will likely need to call a physician's office to get some of the costs. Assume the patient does not have insurance. Tell them it's for a class project.

After you complete the worksheet, in 1 page discuss your findings, including which method you would be inclined to select and why.

Contraception Worksheet

Technique	Yearly cost	STD protection (Y or N)	Typical Failure Rate (%)	Prescription or OTC or N/A	Whose responsible (*man, women, either*)	Convenience in-moment (*good, moderate, poor*)	Comfort (*good, moderate, poor*)
Abstinence Short Description:							
	$120	Y	5%	OTC	Either	good	poor
Pros				Cons			
No Method Short Description:							
	0	N	100%	N/A	Man	poor	moderate
Pros				Cons			
Rhythm Short Description:							
	0	N	90%	N/A	Either	moderate	good
Pros				Cons			
Withdrawal Short Description:							
	100	N	50%	OTC	Man	moderate	poor
Pros				Cons			

Technique	Yearly cost	STD protection (Y or N)	Typical Failure Rate (%)	Prescription or OTC or N/A	Whose responsible (*man, women, either*)	Convenience in-moment (*good, moderate, poor*)	Comfort (*good, moderate, poor*)
Spermicide	Short Description:						
	$90	Y	0%	Prescription	Either	good	good
Pros				Cons			
Sponge	Short Description:						
	$80	N	75%	N/A	Man	good	moderate
Pros				Cons			
Male Condom	Short Description:						
	$50	Y	50%	N/A	Man	moderate	moderate
Pros				Cons			
Female Condom	Short Description:						
	$45	Y	40%	N/A	Women	moderate	moderate
Pros				Cons			
IUD	Short Description:						
	$100	Y	10%	N/A	Either	moderate	poor
Pros				Cons			
Diaphragm	Short Description:						
	$60	Y	5%	N/A	Either	poor	moderate
Pros				Cons			

Technique	Yearly cost	STD protection (Y or N)	Typical Failure Rate (%)	Prescription or OTC or N/A	Whose responsible (*man, women, either*)	Convenience in-moment (*good, moderate, poor*)	Comfort (*good, moderate, poor*)
Hormone Ring	Short Description:						
	$150	Y	5%	OTC	Man	M	G
Pros				Cons			
Hormone Implant	Short Description:						
	$1,500	Y	0%	N/A	Man	G	P
Pros				Cons			
Injections	Short Description:						
	$20	Y	25%	N/A	Man	M	P
Pros				Cons			
The Pill	Short Description:						
	$100	Y	15%	OTC	Woman ~~Either~~	M	G
Pros				Cons			
Patch	Short Description:						
	$40	N	10%	Prescription	Man	P	M
Pros				Cons			
Other: Gel	Short Description:						
	$30	No	10%	Prescription	Man	P	M
Pros				Cons			

Activity 49—Unplanned Pregnancy

Although most pregnancies are planned and wanted, some are unplanned. This could be due to contraception failure, unclear thinking due to substance use, being lost in the moment of passion, or forced intercourse (rape). Without protection, ovulating women have about a 20-25% chance of getting pregnant. Once pregnant, the mother (and father in some cases) has three choices: abort the pregnancy, deliver the child and raise it, or deliver the child and give it up for adoption. This activity will give you some feel for how difficult this decision is and the advantages and disadvantages of each choice.

Directions

Use the questionnaires on the following pages to interview three women regarding their experiences with unplanned pregnancies. One will be with a woman who decided to deliver the child and raise it herself, the second will be with a woman who decided to deliver the child and allow another couple to adopt the child, and the third will be with a woman who decided to abort the pregnancy. It may be difficult to identify these women at first. Perhaps your parents know of women in each category who would be willing to talk about their experiences.

NOTE: This is a sensitive and sometimes even controversial topic. You must exercise empathy and great respect when you speak with these individuals. In-person or telephone interviews would be preferred, but you may do an interview via email if the interviewee prefers.

Once you have completed the interviews, in one page, reflect on what you learned.

Interview #1—Kept Child

Unless you already know the individual, take a few minutes to 'break the ice,' to build a relationship of trust and explain why you want the interview.

◊ Would you be willing to share, in vague terms, how you got pregnant?

◊ Was anyone else influential in your decision to keep the baby? If yes, how?

◊ What were the primary reasons you made this decision?

◊ Talk about what you experienced physically during or after the process?

◊ Talk about what you experienced emotionally during or after the process?

◊ Were your finances affected in any way?

◊ What advice would you give a woman with an un-planned pregnancy?

Interview #2—Let Child be Adopted

Unless you already know the individual, take a few minutes to 'break the ice,' to build a relationship of trust and explain why you want the interview.

◊ Would you be willing to share, in vague terms, how you got pregnant?

◊ Was anyone else influential in your decision to adopt the baby? If yes, how?

◊ What were the primary reasons you made this decision?

◊ Talk about what you experienced physically during or after the process?

◊ Talk about what you experienced emotionally during or after the process?

◊ Were your finances affected in any way?

◊ What advice would you give a woman with an un-planned pregnancy?

Interview #3—Aborted Pregnancy

Unless you already know the individual, take a few minutes to 'break the ice,' to build a relationship of trust and explain why you want the interview.

◊ Would you be willing to share, in vague terms, how you got pregnant?

◊ Was anyone else influential in your decision to abort the pregnancy? If yes, how?

◊ What were the primary reasons you made this decision?

◊ Talk about what you experienced physically during or after the process?

◊ Talk about what you experienced emotionally during or after the process?

◊ Were your finances affected in any way?

◊ What advice would you give a woman with an un-planned pregnancy?

Activity 50—Abortion

Abortion is a term used to refer to the ending of a pregnancy. Spontaneous abortion, also known as miscarriage, is the natural process of a woman's body expelling a fetus that is usually unviable. Abortion can also be induced by a physician at the request of the pregnant woman. The way an abortion is induced varies depending on the number of weeks of pregnancy, the condition of the pregnancy, the condition of the mother, and the preference of the physician. This activity will give you a better understanding of the most common abortion techniques and their related risks.

Directions

Use the following webpages (or other websites) to find information to complete the table that follows.

➤ *http://www.emedicinehealth.com/abortion/page5_em.htm#Explanation%20of%20the%20Procedures*

➤ *http://www.abortionfacts.com/techniques/techniques.asp*

➤ *http://www.nlm.nih.gov/medlineplus/ency/article/002912.htm*

Also, read the article at the following webpage, which discusses the statistics about who has abortions and why they have them.

➤ http://www.guttmacher.org/pubs/psrh/full/3711005.pdf

Then write a one-page reflection on the following questions:

"What are your thoughts about abortion, when, if ever would it be reasonable? "What can be done to reduce the need for and /or the impact of abortion in this country?"

	Weeks Recommended	Potential Risks
Medical (RU-486)	9	steroids
Description:		
Suction Aspiration	7 - 15	pain from vacuuming
Description:		
Dilation & Curettage	6	spreading injection
Dilation & Evacuation	13	surgical instruments inserted into uterous
Description:		
Saline Injection	12	
Description:		
Prostaglandin Injection		
Description:		
Hysterectomy	12	
Description:		
Dilation & Extraction		
Description:		

Part Eleven

End of Life Issues

Activity 51—End of Life Decisions

When illness or injury threatens life, there are often serious decisions to be made about what care to provide, when to stop providing care, and who will make these decisions if the patient is unable to do so. There is a section of law devoted to end of life decisions called Advance Directives. There are 4 primary types of advance directives: (1) Healthcare Directives, (2) Living Wills, (3) Durable Power of Attorney for Health Care (sometimes called Health Care Proxy), and (4) Do Not Resuscitate Orders. Some states laws allow these to be combined into a single document; some do not. Some states require specific language in these documents; some do not. This activity will help you understand some of these issues.

Directions:

1) Get online and read the following short articles about the types of directives and the purposes for which each is intended:

   http://www.nlm.nih.gov/medlineplus/ency/article/001908.htm

   http://www.mayoclinic.com/health/living-wills/HA00014

2) Go to the following web address and look up your state.
   http://www.noah-health.org/en/rights/endoflife/adforms.html

   Under each state is a list of links that discuss the laws regarding advance directives for that state. Read about the rules for your state. (If the webpage is not working, in a web browser, such as *Google* or *Yahoo,* type the words "advance directives" followed by the name of your state. Look for sites that have *.gov* or *.edu* domains.)

3) The site also has links to forms and sample directives. Review the forms and examples given for your state. (Again, if the webpage is not working, browse using the words: "advance directives forms" followed by the name of your state. Look for sites that have *.gov* or *.edu* domains.). Also, visit the following website and read about "Five Wishes," a living will/advance directive template that is popular in many states: *http://www.agingwithdignity.org/five-wishes.php.*

4) After reading the articles and looking at the forms, think about your personal wishes and talk to your family about end-of-life choices. You will may want to consider such things as:

- Who should be proxy if you cannot communicate?

- What to do if death is eminent?

- Under what circumstances not to resuscitate?

- Whether to provide medical assistance such as ventilation, nutrition, hydration, dialysis, blood transfusions, etc.?

- Whether organs and/or tissues will be donated upon death?

- Preferences for body disposition and/or funeral?

5) Ask a local attorney's office what they would charge to prepare the appropriate documents.

6) After careful consideration and discussion, complete the appropriate documents for your state (either through an attorney or by using the free forms and examples). Sign the documents and give copies to family and friends. Also, encourage your family members (particularly older ones) to do the same.

Activity 52—Organ Donation

This activity will help you learn more about organ donation and how it may apply to you and your loved ones.

Directions:

Read the following online articles and answer the questions on the following page:

http://www.organdonor.gov/

http://www.nlm.nih.gov/medlineplus/organdonation.html

http://www.mayoclinic.com/health/organ-donation/FL00077

After reading these articles and completing the worksheet, talk to your family and make a personal decision about organ donation.

<u>Organ Donation Questions</u>

One.   **What percent of those who need organs get them?**

Two.   **Who is not allowed to donate?**

Three.   **What does your religion think about organ donation?**

Four.   **How will organ donation affect a funeral?**

Five.   **What do your family members think about organ donation?**

Six.   **What are your feelings about organ donation?**

Activity 53—Hospice

Hospice is a type of health care given to terminally ill patients with less than 6 months to live. It's a philosophy of palliative care that meets the physical, emotional and, in some cases, spiritual needs of the patient and family. The goal is to preserve dignity, relieve pain for the patient, and reduce stress for the family. Related to hospice care, there are differences in what costs Medicare and various insurance plans with cover. In many markets, hospice is competitive with some for-profit and some non-profit agencies. This activity will give you better understanding of the hospice philosophy, the services available and the related costs.

Directions

I.   Get online and read the following short article about hospice care written by the American Cancer Society:

http://www.cancer.org/docroot/ETO/content/Eto_2_5x_What_Is_Hospice_Care.asp

II.   Next read the following short article regarding what Medicare will cover.

http://www.medicare.gov/publications/pubs/pdf/hosplg.pdf

III. Go to the following website and locate a hospice service in your area:

http://iweb.nhpco.org/iweb/Membership/MemberDirectorySearch.aspx?pageid=3257&showTitle=1

IV.   Call the hospice provider in your home town and ask them the questions on the following page. Tell them you are doing this for a school project. Use the following scenario for your questions:

Your mother has been diagnosed with terminal breast cancer that has metastasized to her bones. Her doctor expects that she has only 2 weeks to live.

She will be staying with you in your home. A family member will be there from 4 pm to 8 am each day, but she will need care during the rest of the day. She is currently cognizant and has agreed to hospice care. You're not sure where to go from this point.

Questions for Hospice

❖ What services would you suggest?

❖ What help will be provided by hospice? And, which functions could the family be trained to provide?

❖ How are decisions such as pain medications and medical sustenance decided?

❖ If these services were provided for 2 weeks, what would be the total cost?

❖ How much would Medicare pay and how much would I pay?

Find a family that has used hospice services sometime in the past. If you do not know of one, ask the hospice provider. Perhaps they know of a family that willing to be contacted. Ask them the following questions. Please be sensitive; feelings may still be close to the surface even if it has been some time since their loved one died. Tell them you are doing this for a class project.

Questions for Family That Used Hospice

❖ Can you tell me briefly why you sought hospice care for your loved one?

❖ Was the family member cared for at home?

❖ What help did they provide the family? And, which functions did the family provide?

❖ Can you tell me how much was not covered by insurance or Medicare?

❖ What advice would you give someone else considering hospice?

Activity 53 continued—Hospice

Activity 54—Assisted Death

Assisted death (suicide) is illegal in most states. However, some believe it should be legal and there are some physicians who will give advice to help a patient painlessly end life without physically assisting the patient. In addition to being a legal issue, this is an ethical issue for many. Which is worse, assisting with the death of another human being or not assisting someone who wants to end suffering? This activity will not answer these questions, but will help you think about some of the issues involved.

Directions:

Read the following case and answer the questions at the end.

Michael Lee was an Air Force transport pilot for 8 years before having a successful career with a major airline. Since retiring 2 years ago, he has enjoyed frequent plane trips to see his daughter and 2 grandsons, teaching flight training part-time at a local airport, and regular rounds of golf. However, he hasn't golfed in sometime because he gets tired quickly and has had increasing pain in his back and side lately. He has also been recovering from pneumonia – the 2ⁿᵈ bout in a year.

After hearing his symptoms, his doctor ordered blood work and an MRI of his spine. Michael was floored by the diagnosis: Multiple Myeloma, *a cancer of the bone marrow that affects white blood cells.*

Treatment for patients his age usually involves high-dose chemotherapy with stem cell transplants. With treatment, about 90% are alive at 2 years. However, most patients have a relapse, the cancer becoming resistant to the treatment. About 1/3 survive to 5 years, and about 1 in 10 live to 10 years.

Michael has always been a proud man. He does not want the pain that will come later in the disease nor the indignity of becoming an emaciated shell of his former self, dependant on others to care for his most basic needs. And, he doesn't want his daughter to shoulder the financial and emotional burden of caring for him, or his grandsons to remember their grandfather this way.

You are Michael's golf buddy and one of his few friends. He approaches you for advice. As a retired pharmacist, you understand that this diagnosis is ultimately terminal and will involve significant suffering toward the end. You also know some ways Michael could quickly, and relatively painlessly, end his life.

Questions

1. What are the ethical issues involved in this case?

2. Is it right for someone to end his or her life by choice? Why or why not?

3. What would you do in this case?

4. What if you were a practicing physician and Michael were a patient not a friend, what would you do?

5. Should assisted death be legal? Why or why not?

6. What if all of Michael's health care were paid by the government; should the government be allowed to refuse his care and let him die? Why or why not?

Activity 55—Funerals

Funerals and body disposition are decisions that many do not fully understand. Overwhelmed by the emotion of the moment, many simply follow the advice of the funeral director without realizing they have choices. In addition to choices for body preparation and disposition, there are choices related to costs. The traditional funeral in the U.S. costs $5-10 thousand, frequently more. This activity will help you better understand the processes and the choices.

Directions:

First. Get online and read the following article about the *Federal Funeral Rule* including a brief summary of the choices and costs:

http://www.ftc.gov/bcp/edu/pubs/consumer/products/pro19.shtm

Second. Research the laws in your state regarding funerals. For example, most states do not have laws requiring vaults for burial, but some cemeteries do. The following link gives an example of a good resource for one state: Georgia. It provides general information and some information specific to Georgia state law:

http://www.lawhelp.org/documents/51811Funeral%20Homes.doc?stateabbrev=/GA/

Third. Complete the following worksheet. To do so, you will likely need to call a local funeral director. Explain that you are doing this survey for a school project; they should be willing to give you the information. You will ask about costs related to the four general choices: A) Traditional full-service funerals with burial, B) Traditional full-services with cremation, C) Immediate burial with or without a memorial service, D) Immediate cremation with or without a memorial service

Fourth. After completing the worksheet, in one page, answer the following questions: 1) What did you learn about the laws, customs, or costs that surprised you? 2) If you had to plan a funeral for a family member next month, which options would you choose and why?

Funeral Options & Costs Worksheet

	Traditional Burial Funeral	Traditional Cremation Funeral	Immediate Burial	Immediate Cremation
SERVICES			$850	850
Removal of body	$2,500	$2500	~~2500~~	2500
Funeral home staff services	$4750	$2000	1950	1475 ~~1475~~
Use of home for viewing	$1095	■	1095	■
Use of home for ceremony	$1500	$1870	1050	1225
Hearse to cemetery	$1950	■	100 ~~1950~~	■
Limousine for family	$4280	$1495	~~1280~~	~~1295~~ 1500 1000

Funeral Options & Costs Worksheet continued

	Traditional Burial Funeral	Traditional Cremation Funeral	Immediate Burial	Immediate Cremation
BODY PREPARATION				
Embalming & cleaning	$1545		680 ~~15~~	
Cosmetology & dressing	$2500		1100 ~~700~~	
Cremation		$5700		$3500
CASKET				
Loaner for services	$3455		1700 ~~3800~~	
Burial bag only	$135		50 ~~50~~	
Cloth covered casket	$3455		~~~~ 1050	
Steel casket	$2495		~~~~ 1500	
Hardwood casket	$2000		~~2000~~ 1000	
Decorative urn		$400		$550 ~~~~ 150
Inexpensive urn		$100		$100 20
CEMETARY				
Opening & closing hole	$1450		850 ~~1450~~	
Plot	$1500		950 ~~1500~~	
Vault	$1,100		900 ~~1,100~~	
Temporary headstone	500 ~~$20~~		25 ~~50~~	
Permanent monument	$5000		~~5000~~ 500	

Funeral Options & Costs Worksheet continued

	Traditional Burial Funeral	Traditional Cremation Funeral	Immediate Burial	Immediate Cremation
OTHER				
Flowers	$50	$50	$15	$15
Announcements, cards, etc	$225	$200	$50	$50
Food & drink	$500	$450	$150	$100
Obituary, death certificate	$25	$20	$10	$5
Minister honorarium	$225	$150	$75	$50
Other:				
TOTAL COST	$1025	$870	$300	$220

Part Twelve

Insurance

Activity 56—Private Health Insurance

Lately, there has been a great deal of interest in the rising cost of health insurance. Many individuals obtain their health insurance coverage through their employers or the government. However, others are self-employed or work at places that do not offer health insurance. They must seek insurance on their own. This activity will expose you to insurance options and their associated costs.

Directions:

With this assignment, you will compare two different health insurance policies. To do this, you will need to contact local insurance agencies. You can contact single provider agencies or insurance brokers, as long as you meet the assignment criteria. One policy must be an HMO-type (must see organization's doctor) or PPO-type policy (list of preferred providers), the other must be a high-deductible/low-premium policy (for example one with an annual deductible of $1000-1500). Use the following scenario:

Dad—39, Mom—37, Son—9, and Daughter—5. Assume everyone is in good health with no known pre-existing conditions, except the Son is taking Ritalin. You are seeking an individual family policy because Dad and Mom are self-employed in the family business. If an agent starts asking too many specific questions, explain that this is a school project.

1) After identifying the companies, complete the short tables that follow for each policy. You can do this by telling the agent you have an insurance comparison worksheet from which you would like to ask him/her some questions. Alternatively, you could have the agent send you a policy brochure and look up the answers yourself (this will require some lead time).

Worksheet—What does the policy cover?

Directions: *Simply check if the policy covers the particular type of care.*

	HMO or PPO	High Deductible	No insurance
Name of policy			✕
Hospital care	✗	✓	✕
Inpatient surgery		✓	✕
Outpatient surgery		✓	✕
Doctor office visits	✓		✕
Birth control	✓		✕
Maternity care		✓	✕
Well-baby care		✓	✕
Immunizations	✓		✕
Mammograms	✓		✕
x-rays and other imaging	✓		✕
Dental care	✓		✕
Orthodontic care	✓		✕
TMJ		✓	✕
Vision care	✓		✕
Prescriptions	✓		✕
Long-term nursing care		✓	✕
Pre-existing Conditions		✓	✕

Worksheet—What is the policy's...?

Directions: *Write the amount in dollars.* A premium *is what policy holders pay annually for the policy.* A deductible *is the amount that they must pay annually before the insurance pays anything.* Co-payment *is a flat dollar amount that they must pay every time they have a health care visit.* Co-insurance *is similar to co-payment except it is a percentage not a set dollar amount. Most companies require either a co-payment or co-insurance, but not both.* Out-of-pock max, *as the name implies, is the maximum you must pay in a year before the insurance pays 100% of the remaining costs for the year. Some companies also set* limits *on how much they are willing to pay* annually *or in the* lifetime *of the policy.*

	HMO or PPO	High Deductible	No insurance
Name of policy			
Annual premium	$1 2985	$ 1500	
Extra premium for maternity if not already covered	$1060		
Annual individual deductible	$1 300		
Annual family deductible	600		
Co-payment (flat rate) per incident	$ 10		
Co-insurance (percentage) per incident	20%		
Annual Family "out of pocket" cap (max)	5000		
Lifetime limit on coverage	$ 2400		
Annual limits on coverage (amounts of services)	$ 1500		

2) For each policy, complete the following spreadsheets for the three scenarios. To do this, you will need to:

   a. calculate whether each annual, individual and/or family deductible has been met for each policy (where applicable).

   b. calculate the amount of co-insurance (if any) to be paid for each policy.

   c. total all the deductibles for each event.

   d. after completing each worksheet, determine what percent of the total medical expenses the family is responsible for under each scenario for each policy (remember some policies have "out of pocket" caps).

   e. then, add the total medical care expenses to the annual premium for each plan in each scenario.

Scenario I— Nothing Unusual		HMO or PPO plan			High Deductible plan			No insurance
		to co-pay	*to deductible*	*to co-insurance*	*to co-pay*	*to deductible*	*to co-insurance*	
Dad	Physical [$100]	$20	$10	$10	$10	$10	$10	$50
Mom	Flu Visit [$75]	20	10	10	10	10	10	$25
	Birth Control Prescription [6 mo @ $15 = $90]	15	10	10	15	15	10	$40
Son	Stitches [$150]	25	15	10	20	15	15	75
	Ritalin prescription [12 mo @ $20 = $240]	30	20	15	30	25	20	100
Daughter	Ear infection [$75]	15	15	10	10	15	15	20
	Antibiotics [$50]	15	10	10	10	15	10	20
Subtotal each category of medial expense		140	90	75	105	105	90	330
Total all 3 categories of medical expenses (or *out of pocket limit*, if reached)		305			300			330
Total premiums for year		780 + 3660			780 + 3600			780 + 3960
Grand total expenses plus premiums		4440			4380			4740

Scenario 2— New Baby		HMO or PPO plan			High Deductible plan			No insurance
		to co-pay	to deductible	to co-insurance	to co-pay	to deductible	to co-insurance	
Dad	Physical [$100]	20	10	10	10	10	10	50
Mom	Pregnancy [18 visits or labs @$100 = $1800]	500	250	250	250	125	125	1500
	Delivery--OB [$6,000]	2700	1000	500	1500	1000	750	4500
	Birth Control Prescription [3 mo@$15 = $45]	10	10	10	10	10	10	25
Son	Stitches [$150]	25	15	10	20	15	15	75
	Ritalin prescription [12 mo@$20 = $240]	30	20	15	30	25	20	100
Daughter	Ear infection [$75]	15	15	10	10	15	15	20
	Antibiotics [$50]	15	10	10	10	15	10	20
Subtotal each category of medial expense		3315	1330	815	1840	1215	955	6290
Total all 3 categories of medical expenses (or out of pocket limit, if reached)		5460			4010			6290
Total premiums for year		8460 + 65520			8460 + 48120			8460 + 75480
Grand total expenses plus premiums		73 980			56 580			83940

Scenario 3— Heart Attack		HMO or PPO plan			High Deductible plan			No insurance
		to co-pay	to deductible	to co-insurance	to co-pay	to deductible	to co-insurance	
Dad	Heart attack ER visit [$12,000]	6000	3000	3500	4000	2000	2000	8000
	Bypass Surgery [$50,000]	25000	12500	12500	15000	7500	7000	30,000
	Cardiac Rehab [$2,000]	1000	500	500	750	500	250	1500
Mom	Flu Visit [$75]	20	10	10	10	10	10	25
	Birth Control Prescription [6 mo@$15 = $90]	10	10	10	10	10	10	25
Son	Stitches [$150]	25	15	10	20	15	15	75
	Ritalin prescription [12 mo@$20 = $240]	30	20	15	30	25	20	100
Daughter	Ear infection [$75]	15	15	10	10	15	15	20
	Antibiotics [$50]	15	10	10	10	15	10	20
Subtotal each category of medial expense		32115	16080	16565	19840	10090	9330	39765
Total all 3 categories of medical expenses (or out of pocket limit, if reached)		64760			39260			39765
Total premiums for year		64680			64680			64680
Grand total expenses plus premiums		129,440			103 940			104445

3) After completing all the worksheets, answer the following questions:

- Which was the best policy under each scenario?

  The best policy under each scenario is the high deductible plan.

- What are the advantages and disadvantages of each policy?

  The advantages of each policy is that prices vary among the case, disadvantages would be the amount you have to pay.

- If these three scenarios happened back-to-back, which policy would be the best across all three years?

  The policy that would be the best across all three years is high deductible plan.

- Having done this research, which policy would you opt for if you were in this family's circumstances? Why?

  I would choose the HMO or PPO plan because the lower prices for the high deductible plan could have hidden fees that still need to be paid.

Activity 57—Long-term Care

Toward the end of life more than half of adults will need long-term nursing care. Some of this care will be related to medical services. However, some will be related to activities of daily living such as dressing, bathing, toileting, eating, walking, etc. Although many of the medical services are covered by *Medicare* or private health insurance, assistance with daily living activities is not covered. This activity will help you better understand typical long-term care needs, options, and associated costs.

Directions:

1) Read this short article from the *National Center for Assisted Living*:

   http://www.longtermcareliving.com/financial_information/insurance1.htm.

2) Visit this website and read about what *Medicare* will pay:

   http://www.medicare.gov/LongTermCare/Static/Home.asp

3) After reading the articles, complete the worksheet that follows. You will need to contact local, long-term care service providers to learn the typical cost of the various services in your area. You will find rates for three different types of services: semi-private nursing home, home health aide, and adult day services.

	Cost per day	Cost for 1 year
Semi-private room in nursing home	$ 189	$ 68,985
Home health aide from 8am to 6pm	$310	$ 113,150
Adult day services from 8am to 6pm	$100	$ 36,500

4) You will also need to contact one or more long-term care insurance providers in your area (if no local agents offer these type of insurance products, try these online sites for quotes: _shttp://click-trak.com/rds/forms/insure/_ OR _http://www.intelliquote.com/longtermcare/_). To get an accurate quote, you will need to provide them some information. Use the following scenario:

Use your gender. You are currently 65 years old, widowed, and living at home. You are 5'9" and weigh 185 lbs. Your health is average; you have osteoarthritis and are taking medication to control your blood pressure. You want insurance that will cover you for up to 3 year of long-term care. You would also like inflation protection. They will also ask about how much daily (or monthly) benefit you will require. To get this information, use the rate given for a local nursing home, semi-private room. (determine how the rate would change if you were 75 instead of 65 or if you had unlimited length of coverage)

	Yearly premium if purchased at age 65	Yearly premium if purchased at age 75
3 year length of coverage	$2902	$1368
Unlimited length of coverage	$3150	$2400

5) After completing the worksheets, in one page, discuss what you found and what option you would likely choose if your father or mother needed assistance while you were gone to work.

Activity 58—Life Insurance

Life insurance is not really a health issue, but a financial instrument. However, the policy holder's health has dramatic effect on the types of life insurance that are available and the costs associated with acquiring them. Most people who buy life insurance do so because they will leave behind dependents or a spouse who will be affected by the loss of their income, by estate taxes, burial costs or other costs associated with their death.

There are three primary classes of life insurance: Accidental Death/Dismemberment (AD&D), Permanent, and Term. AD&D insurance is usually the least expensive but only pays if death is due to an accident (not illness). It also usually offers partial benefit if you lose a limb, eyesight or hearing. The similarity among all types of Permanent life insurance (e.g., whole, universal, variable) is that they all last the entire life of the policy holder, no matter how long he/she lives. Most Permanent policies also provide cash payouts or various investment options.

Term life is usually less expensive than Permanent, does not have investment options, and cannot be cashed in while living. Term life simply pays the face value of the policy if the policy holder dies for any reason (except suicide) during the term of the policy (usually 10, 20, 30, or 40 years).

This activity will focus on Term life insurance because it is easier to understand and is a pure death benefit instrument. Most policy holders can usually approximate the advantage of an entire-life policy (without all the cashing or investment options), by selecting a 40-year term with level premiums. For this activity, you will learn about the cost of acquiring Term life insurance and how various health issues and lifestyle choices can affect the cost.

Directions:

I. Read over the following table. This will give you an idea what insurance actuaries have calculated to be the greatest risks for death. A *Preferred Plus* rating requires almost perfect health and lifestyle.

Term Life Health Rating Classes	Preferred Plus (best)	Preferred	Standard
Alcohol/Substance Abuse			✓
Arthritis (Osteo)		✓	✓
Asthma (allergy)		✓	✓
Asthma (steroid meds)			✓
Cancer (after 5 years) (except basal cell OK)			✓
Heart Disease			not available
Depression (on going)			✓
Diabetes			not available
Emphysema			not available
Epilepsy			✓
Hepatitis (A,B)		✓	✓
Hepatitis (C)			not available
Kidney or Liver Disease			not available
Mental Illness			not available
Multiple Sclerosis			not available
Stroke			not available
Ulcerative Colitis			✓
Vascular Disease			not available
Blood Pressure	<140/85	<150/90	<155/95
Cholesterol	<230	<250	<300
Tobacco Use	None last 5 years	None last 3 years	None last year
Driving Record	None past 3 years & no DUI last 5 years	None past 3 years & no DUI last 5 years	None past 3 years & no DUI last 2 years
Family History	No parents or siblings *diagnosed* with heart disease/ cancer <60 years old	No parents or siblings *died* of heart disease/ cancer <60 years old	Not Applicable

II. Get on the internet; use one of the following websites to calculate a premium for term life insurance: *http://www.intelliquote.com/* OR *http://www.quickquote.com/getaqq.html*

III. You will have to enter certain information into a form (give a fake name and contact information, unless you are sincerely interested in being contacted by a representative). Use the following scenario:

State:	your own
Gender:	your own
Height:	5'9"
Tobacco:	never
Amount:	$1,000,000
Term:	30 years
Premium:	look for annual

You will calculate the rate 18 times, changing certain variables each time:

Age:	30	50	70
Weight:	160 lbs	210 lbs	
Health rating:	Preferred Plus	Preferred	Standard

V. As you calculate the premiums, complete the table that follows.

How do age, health and weight affect Term life premiums?

Age	Weight	Health Rating		
		Preferred+	Preferred	Standard
30 years old	160 lbs	728 8736	938 11256	1518 -15 18216
	210 lbs	1318 15816	1318 15816	1518 18216
50 years old	160 lbs	3068 $36816	3958 47496	6238 74856
	210 lbs	4798 57576	3965 47580	6238 74856
70 years old	160 lbs	2018 24216	2181 26172	2687 32244
	210 lbs	2181 26172	2181 26172	2687 32244

Use yearly premiums.

V. After you have completed the table, in one page, discuss what you learned, what surprised you, and what you will likely do with regard to life insurance when you are in a life stage to have dependents.

Part Thirteen

Consumer Protection

Activity 59—Federal Agencies for Health Fraud

Two federal agencies are primarily responsible for protecting consumers from health-related fraud or harm: *The Federal Trade Commission (FTC)* and the *Food and Drug Administration (FDA)*. Both have the authority to reprimand, fine, and prosecute offenders if necessary.

The FTC monitors companies and enforces laws in industries related to consumer products, credit/loans, energy, investments, communications, theft and health. It divides health issues into devices, procedures, weight loss, and supplements.

The FDA, by law, has oversight for food, drugs, medical devices, cosmetics, veterinary products/procedures, vaccines/biologicals, tobacco, and dietary supplements. It approves new products and monitors the use of existing products or procedures.

This activity will allow you to observe some of the activities of these two agencies.

Directions

Federal Trade commission (FTC)

a) Read the short article about the function of FTC at the following webpage: *http://www.ftc.gov/bcp/about.shtm*

b) Go to the following webpage that has a list of companies that have been party to FTC action. All of the cases involved some type of dietary supplement. Select one case that sounds interesting to you. *http://www.ftc.gov/bcp/reports/dietadvertisingcases.shtm*

c) Move to the following webpage: *http://www.ftc.gov/opa/.* In the search box at the top right, type the name of the company or product mentioned in the case. Then, click on and read the press release about the case.

d) Complete the table that follows, including a brief summary of why the company was cited and what action the FTC took, including any fines.

Example of FTC Action	
Name of Company	Snore Formula, Inc.
Name of Product	Snore Formula
Purpose of Product	preventing people from snoring a lot, reduces snoring.
Reason for Action	Many people snore too much and it becomes difficult when people are trying to sleep around that person
Type of Action including fines	A consent agreement is for settlement purposes only and does not constitute an admission of a law violation. When the Commission issues a consent order on a final basis, it carries the force of law w/ respect to future actions. Each violation of such an order may

result in a civil penalty of $11,000.

Consumer Health Activities

Food and Drug Administration (FDA)

a) Read the short article about the purpose of the FDA with regard to dietary supplements at the following webpage: *http://www.fda.gov/Food/DietarySupplements/ConsumerInform ation/ucm110417.htm#regulate*

b) Move to the following webpage: *http://www.accessdata.fda.gov/scripts/warningletters/wlSearch Result.cfm?qryStr=&Search=Search*

In the search box, part way down the page in the center, type the word "supplement." The search will generate a list of hundreds of companies that have been party to FDA action with regard to their supplements.

c) Select one that sounds interesting to you and click on the name for a full description of the case. In the table that follows, briefly summarize the case.

Example of FDA Action	
Name of Company	21st Century Sports Nutritionals, Inc.
Name of Product	Phenylkinetics
Purpose of Product	Intended for stimulating sexual interest and function and/or for weight loss.

Example of FDA Action cont.							
Reason for Action	Marketed as a drug	Contains unapproved drug	Mis-branded	Mis-labeled	Unsubstantiated claims	Function or structure not supported	Contains adulterated product
(check all that apply)		✓			✓		✓
Examples to support action	Phenylkinetics contains norephedrone HCI, which does not give an energy boost and makes you not hungry, but you have to remind yourself to eat.						
Type of Action including fines	Correct the violations. Failing to correct violations result in enforcement action. Seizure of illegal products and for injunction against the manufacturer and/or distributor of illegal products.						

Activity 60—Health Ethics

Sometimes, questions regarding health are not as simple as one correct response or choice. Often, there are conflicting choices with advantages and disadvantages. And, choosing among these choices can present ethical dilemmas for patients, care givers, educators, government agencies and law makers. Ethics is an attempt to formalize morality, finding ways to agree on what is right and wrong. Following government commissions to investigate unethical practices, such as the Tuskegee Syphilis study, the Belmont report was issued in 1979, outlining a few fundamental ethical principles. Other principles have been added since, including those listed below:

Autonomy—*Individual agency. The right of individuals to govern their own lives and have the agency to make personal decisions shall be respected unless their decisions put others at risk.*

Beneficence—*Do good. Those in positions to provide care or assistance to an individual should do so to the degree that is reasonably possible.*

Justice—*Be fair. Those in positions of care giving or power, including government, should treat individuals equitably and equally as much as is feasible.*

Non-Malfeasance—*Do no harm. Caregivers and those in position of power have a responsibility to prevent harm to patients or citizens.*

Truth—*Be honest. Don't knowingly lie or deceive; and, take steps to assure that individuals will learn and understand the truth.*

Confidentiality—*Respect individual privacy and take steps to protect private information.*

Directions:

a) Read the definitions of the bioethical principles on the previous page. Dilemmas occur when two are more principles are in conflict with each other.

b) Consider each of the potential ethical dilemmas listed in the table that follows. Add an additional dilemma of your choosing. Place check marks in the boxes, indentifying principles that are in conflict.

c) Decide whether you are in favor or against the listed practice. Circle the check mark(s) for the principle(s) that carried the greatest weight in your decision.

POTENTIAL ETHICAL DILEMMAS	Autonomy	Beneficence	Justice	Non-Malfeasance	Truth	Confidentiality
Abortion	✓					
Using fear tactics to get kids not to try marijuana		✓				
Economic means tests for getting Medicare					✓	
Publishing names of individuals who are HIV+						✓
Testing an HIV vaccine in poor prostitutes in Africa				✓		
Euthanasia	✓					
Mandatory helmets for motorcycle riders		✓				
Programs to encourage sterilization for unfit parents		✓				
Physician assisted death			✓			
Other:						

d) Choose one practice for which you had a difficult time making a decision. Argue both sides of the issue using the following table.

Ethical Pros and Cons

Practice: Choosing a Restaurant

Arguments for Practice	Counter Arguments
- Good looking food - cheap food	- unhealthy - no quality

Activity 60 continued—Health Ethics

Index

LaVergne, TN USA
19 September 2010
197649LV00003B/1/P